And They Ask Me
Why I Drink?

Nino "THE GREASEMAN" *Mannelli*

And They Ask Me Why I Drink?

POCKET BOOKS

New York   London   Toronto   Sydney   Tokyo   Singapore

DISCLAIMER

This book is funny. The Greaseman is dealing with only a limited grasp on reality and anything he says must be taken with a grain of salt. As his psychiatrist says, the guy is nuts, grab him.

POCKET BOOKS, a division of Simon & Schuster Inc.
1230 Avenue of the Americas, New York, NY 10020

ISBN: 0-671-55160-4

First Pocket Books hardcover printing November 1997

10 9 8 7 6 5 4 3 2 1

Printed in the U.S.A.

To Anita

Who astonishes me with her beauty,
Dazzles me with her smile,
And keeps me warm with her love—
And she ain't a bad cook either!

Acknowledgments

First of all, I'd like to thank Len Sherman, who had the unsavory task of making heads and tails out of the gloppy pages I gave him . . . nice job with my rantings and ravings . . .

To Sue Carswell, for picking up the phone and getting the book started, and for editing the first draft . . . I'll save that marked-up copy forever. "Grease, what the hell is, what fer?" You've been in New York too long, Sue . . .

Many thanks to Jeff Davis for being my secret weapon, and to Bill Scanlon, Joel Thatcher, Tom Lange, Steve Lucas, and Marcia Shipley for keeping me on top of my game.

My undying love and gratitude to my mom and dad for encouraging me, even as a bald-faced boy, to go for it.

Thanks to Uncle Mel for turning my show loose on the world.

And to Brian Dennehy and Michael Talbott—thanks for being there when it counted.

Contents

Contents

And They Ask Me
Why I Drink?

CALLER: *I've been listening to this show for weeks and I still haven't figured out what the point is.*

GREASEMAN: *That's because there is no point, other than hopefully to make you laugh. This show is a reflection of life, sir, and life is completely pointless!*

Prologue:

Greetings from the Greaseman

Think about it. Think of the gadzillion-to-one odds that created us. Like it or not, here we are. We go through life, getting wrinkles in our brain from studying and working. We labor away with some sort of dream of family, or financial independence, or—dare I say it?—happiness.

Ha! You think you have a chance? Think again! Consider, if you will, the pharaohs of ancient Egypt. They thought they were great. Hey, they *were* great! They commanded millions of citizens. They dominated the ancient world. They built gigantic pyramids to commemorate their lives, to attest to their worthiness. They sought immortality through architecture. Amazingly, those monuments still stand. However, outside of a handful of archaeologists and the director of the British Museum, how many people can name three of them? Can you? Me neither!

Today the pyramids have been reduced to huge photo props. Big-bellied tourists in multicolored Hawaiian shirts and khaki shorts stand gazing into the hot desert sand, their hands cupped over their eyes, awaiting their turn on top of the camel for the obligatory goofy picture. They take pictures of the surrounding souvenir stands and drip trails of hotdog mustard as they stumble around the crumbling stones. They reflect not on the glories of these noble kings and their far-flung kingdoms, but on the vision of a tall, cold one back at the hotel bar.

My point? There was no point, not even for the greatest of monarchs! The pharaohs were here, they lived, they died. If they were really lucky, they died suddenly of a severe myocardial infarction. No fuss, no muss: Bing! If not, they rotted away while their families wept at their bedsides, during the off-hours that they weren't busily laying claim to the royal possessions.

So what point could a radio show possibly have, other than to be merely a diversion along the path of life?

I, host of all hosts, am here for those moments when you realize that everything is pointless. It is at those times, knowing you're another step closer to the grave, that your arteries are hardening, that your life is simply a count-down of heartbeats, that you can pop me on and say, "Well, might as damn well have a laugh, shan't I?"

So come to me when the enormity of this fact sinks in, and I shall make you laugh. Still, you have to give of yourself to my show and, now, to my book. I don't just hand the laughs over to you on a silver platter. I don't just announce, "Here they are."

No, you've got to cock your head, like a Doberman listening to a distant whistle. You've got to apply what you've learned in life to the nuances fed to you on these pages, so that you can come away with a warm sense of contribution. You must use your mental signet ring to understand exactly what's going on. So pay attention, pay strict attention, because we're in this together. Everything that I have to tell you is everything you need to hear. Nothing superfluous, nothing extra. Every word, when employed by a renowned storyteller such as yours truly, is here for a reason. Allow the following story to demonstrate.

Noah Webster, the great lexicographer, spent years hunched over his desk, assiduously working on his famous dictionary. He labored in quiet solitude, alone in his chambers, apart from his wife and the pretty, young housekeeper who helped dust, clean, and cook.

Everything was going along just fine until one afternoon the housekeeper interrupted his work. "Noah," she said, entering his inner sanctum. "I brought you some nice tea and crumpets."

Webster looked up from his writing desk and suddenly jumped to his feet. The difficulty and loneliness of his work had finally gotten to him. He swept his desk clean, knocking everything on the floor, and grabbed the housekeeper. "I've wanted you since you first came to work here! I need you! I am hungry, but not for crumpets! I'm hungry for *you!*" He threw her on the desk and began hobbling her with a passion previously unknown to him.

They were in the midst of ingus when his wife unexpectedly entered the room. "Oh my God, Noah," she cried, "I am surprised!"

"No, my dear," Webster replied. "You are *astonished!* I am *surprised!*"

Of course, my extraordinary grasp of our common language doesn't change the fundamental peculiarity and weirdness of our existence. It's a strange world, and you've got to be prepared.

Let me give you an example.

And They Ask Me Why I Drink?

An ordinary woman worked at her ordinary office job. While enjoying her morning coffee at work one day, she accidentally spilled a few drops down the front of her dress. Though she was upset about the stain, she waited until lunch before heading home to change into something else.

The woman was more than a bit surprised when she drove up to her house and found her husband's car parked in the driveway, since she expected him to be at work. She was even more puzzled when she went inside the house and heard a cracking sound coming from the bedroom.

The woman walked down the hall to the bedroom. The door was open and she could see a naked ten-year-old boy. His ankles and wrists were shackled to the four-poster bed, and red welts covered his entire body. Her husband was standing atop the bed with a whip in his hand. He was naked as well, except for a black leather mask.

As the woman stood there, stunned, horrified, not knowing what to do, her husband whacked the kid with the whip. Then her husband bent down and took a massive on the kid's chest.

That did it. Unable to contain herself any longer, the woman marched into the bedroom. "Harold!" she yelled. "What in the blue blazes is going on here?"

Whip in hand, Harold slowly turned to face her. He looked at her for a moment, then coolly replied, "Nothing much, dear. I just thought I'd take a *sick day!*"

Think about it. Give yourself over to the irrefutable pointlessness of it all. Ponder the pain. Enjoy. Giggle. Laugh.

It's my duty to help you along your journey through life.

A young man, a college student, called in to my show one afternoon. He was seriously considering majoring in communications—imagining that he, too, could be a Big

Boss Jock—and he asked me what I believed were the necessary ingredients for a successful career in radio.

Without having to ponder the question, I replied, "Life and all the experiences it offers."

It's true. Life and all its experiences have made me the man I am and have given me my own particular wry bent on life. It's the difficulties of existing on this planet that have given me the wherewithal and the gumption to move forward. Seeing what I've seen, being blessed with what I've been blessed, and avoiding what I've avoided—all that has made me a man just happy to be here.

Of course, a licensed shrink might speculate that my wacky brand of comedy is actually nothing more than a defense mechanism against the pain I've suffered over the years, and that the grotesquely muscular body I've encased myself in is the subliminal end result of past humiliations.

And that shrink just might be right.

Truthfully, I don't know what I'd do if I were in another profession. For me, this job is therapy. It keeps me sane. I think I'd probably be sitting in the corner of a rubber room somewhere, naked and drooling, if I didn't have this show.

I know you see me as the perky Boss Jock, answering callers' questions with great aplomb and wisdom, spinning stories, singing songs, duck-walking, and strumming my guitar. I know you accept without question my image as a Diddy-bopping Daddy of the Airwaves. I realize you envy my lifestyle, and my fertile, agile, and creative mind. You admire the wit and the originality I pour into The Greaseman Show on a daily basis.

Though I am humbled by your worship, I wasn't always the lumbering Diddy-bopping Daddy I am today. Like all of you, I have been shaped by my experiences. Now is your chance to learn of them, to grasp the extent to which I am a product of my environment. You'll realize the toll a dysfunctional family can take on a sensitive, callow youth such as I once was. You'll grasp the significance of the suffering I have endured, how the arrows of outrageous misfortune penetrated my heart and my mind—especially those hurled at me by my first wife, that pig, Estelle. You'll slowly fathom the cruel depravity of the battles I've fought and the obstacles I've overcome as I've traveled the path of life, from a bald-faced boy to a Big Time Boss Jock. Ultimately, you will comprehend why it is written in my station contract that I *must* visit the psychiatrist each week!

In other words, I don't just have one skeleton in my closet, I've got a whole graveyard in there.

Nevertheless, I will tell you everything. I will share every triumphant moment and every hideous episode. And why am I doing this? Because I have a dream. It is a simple dream, really; a modest dream. My dream is that the circumstances of my life will serve as an inspiration to those among you who are suffering now. All I ask in return for my candor is that you be tender and not laugh in my face. Be kind with the knowledge I am about to impart, the piece of me I am freely giving you, for now you will finally know the answer to the question asked me so often.

Yes, by the time you finish absorbing the wit, the philosophy, and the insights spread across the following pages, YOU WILL KNOW WHY I DRINK!

Part I

Portrait of the Grease as a Young Man

CALLER: *Grease, you're nuts. Do you attribute this to childhood trauma?*

GREASEMAN: *I don't know, but I'll tell this much: My parents kept me in a crib with legs six feet off the ground, so they could hear when I fell out of bed. So to answer your question—your guess is as good as mine!*

Chapter 1

Childhood Memories

I often think my life is just a collection of stories, sometimes strange and wondrous, stories that perhaps taught me more than any boy needs to know. One of my earliest memories involves my dear Grandma and Grandpa. I was staying at their house, and my room was next to the bathroom. I can still close my eyes and recall the sound of Grandpa's slippers shuffling across the hardwood floor on his way to the john in the middle of the night.

On this particular occasion, I heard Grandpa shuffle into the bathroom. I lay in bed and waited, and waited, but I didn't hear him shuffle back to bed. Concerned, I climbed out of bed and crept to the bathroom door, which was open a crack. I peered inside and there was my beloved Grandpa. He was just standing there, staring down at himself, and muttering.

9

And They Ask Me Why I Drink?

"All these years," he was saying, "you've performed for me on cue, and now I stand here in the bathroom for the simplest of tasks and you let me down."

Just then Grandma yelled from the bedroom, "Horace, who in the world are you talking to in there?"

"No one *you'd* remember!" Grandpa yelled back.

With all the violence, the craziness, and the political correctness rampant in society these days, I often yearn to go back to those days of my youth when people were seemingly normal. Serial killers weren't on the prowl, murders were few and far between, and doors remained unlocked without fear of burglars and rapists. People spoke kindly to each other—even to strangers.

In fact, when I was just a bald-faced little boy, my great-grandfather Mannelli would often recall stories of freighters who braved the elements to deliver everything from cloth to tools to molasses to rural America. Freighters were the men who drove a horse and wagon across the land delivering the goods that made people's lives better and easier, goods that helped make this country grow. You can imagine the joy of the locals whenever a freighter, his wagon stacked with exciting new merchandise, arrived in town.

One of Great-Grandpa's favorite stories was about a freighter who was driving his team to Little Rock one dark night when the weather suddenly turned ugly. It was a real bad storm, with rain that turned the ground to mud and lightning that shot through the sky and struck the earth with a terrifying force.

In the distance, the freighter saw a house. The lights were on and smoke curled out of the chimney. A more warm and inviting sight the poor, wet man could not conceive. The freighter pulled over, went up to the door, and asked if he could spend the night. Back in those good old days, people would gladly take in a stranger. They'd look around and say, "Shouldn't be out on a night like this!"

The couple invited the freighter in. They took his wet slicker and sat him down by the fire where they served him a meal. When it came time to turn in, the couple even invited the freighter to share their bed. Beds were big and, hell, more bodies meant more warmth. Back then, people did that kind of thing. So the freighter got into bed and everybody promptly fell asleep. Well, almost everybody.

As the freighter started drifting into a deep sleep, the wife elbowed him awake. "My husband's asleep," she whispered. "Let's have at it!" Not one to turn down a free meal or a good deal, the freighter decided, "Why not?" He began putting the stones to the wife.

Right in the middle of hobbling the woman, the freighter saw that the farmer was up and watching this unexpected event. The freighter thought real fast and began making noises as though he was driving his team, hoping that the farmer would think he was just having a dream.

"Hup, Nellie!" he said. "Hup! Hup! Nellie! Hup! Hup! Hup!"

The farmer listened to this for a minute then raised himself up on one elbow. He looked over at the freighter and said, "Stranger, it looks like you're going to have to dump your load to get out of that mudhole!!"

Ah, yes, the good old days. There was a trust, a naïveté that no longer exists. People these days are worried about everything and it's driving them nuts, turning them into full-fledged candidates for nervous breakdowns. When I was young, the only thing I was concerned with was getting through the day without being called on by the teacher. That was my terror—contemplating having to stand up in class, knees knocking, while the teacher asked me one hideous question after another. Teachers used to do exactly that: teach by intimidation. You studied just in case you were called on, to spare yourself the gruesome embarrassment of ignorance.

I remember when my fifth-grade teacher walked into the classroom and said, "Okay, children, it's pop quiz time! Who said 'Give me liberty or give me death?'" We all sat in silence until, finally, this little Japanese kid in our class stood up and said, "Patrick Henry! 1774!"

The teacher looked around the classroom in disbelief. "Now isn't that something," she exclaimed. "This little boy comes over to this country with his hard-working family. They don't even know the language yet. And still their son knows American history better than any of you. That should make you all feel terrible."

Just then a tiny voice from the back of the classroom yelled, "Screw the Japanese!" The teacher angrily whirled around. "Who said that?" she asked, her eyes darting from face to face. Suddenly the same voice yelled out, "Harry Truman! 1945!"

Yes, take me back to a simpler time, like those years when I was sitting there at PS32 in the heart of the Bronx, a fresh-faced schoolboy loving life. You see, I wasn't always the languid, depleted man you see now, finding solace, blessed relief, in a bottle. There was a time when I had hopes of a bright and promising tomorrow. There was a time when, instead of sitting back in a surly manner, I would eagerly participate.

I remember when I was about ten or eleven years old, the teacher announced, "Mother's Day is coming up. Who would like to write what your mother likes best on the blackboard?"

I was the first one out of my chair, waving my hands and yelling, "I would, I would!"

The teacher said, "Okay, Nino, come on up here." I ran up to the front of the classroom, and she handed me the chalk. I turned to the blackboard and I carefully began to write "F-U-C—."

All of a sudden, the teacher jumped up from her desk and grabbed the chalk out of my hand. "Good God, young man! Just what were you going to write on that blackboard?"

"What my Mom likes best," I replied. "Fuchsia flowers."

"Oh," she said. "Well, in that case, continue to write."

I winked at the teacher. "Mom likes what you thought I was going to write *second best!*"

It was during that same school year that I learned a story can have a moral, a lesson that has served me well in my career.

"Children," the teacher said, "a moral is when you learn what's right and what's wrong through behavior. Does everyone here understand what I just said?"

Before anyone could answer, a little kid in the back of the class stood up. "Teacher, I think I know what a moral is. My mommy told me never to cross the street unless you're at the corner and you see a green light. I never understood why until my friend Johnny crossed between two cars in the middle of the street and got hit. So I guess the moral of that story is that your parents do know what's best."

The teacher smiled. "That's very good," she said proudly. "You do understand it."

And They Ask Me Why I Drink?

Next a little girl in the front of the class stood. "I think I've got one, too, teacher," she said. "Last night at dinner my brother and I were messing around and I knocked over my milk. Since the glass was in front of my little brother I was thinking of blaming it on him so I wouldn't get yelled at. But I didn't. I said, 'I spilled my milk, Mommy, and I'll clean it up.' And Mommy said, 'It's good that you admitted it. And after you clean it up you can have an extra cookie for dessert!'

"So I guess the moral of that," said the little girl, "is to always tell the truth."

When she'd finished her story, I stood up. "I think I understand," I said.

The teacher smiled. "What is your story with a moral, Nino?"

"My daddy stormed the beaches at Normandy in World War II," I began. "There was heavy resistance so Daddy dove into a foxhole. All he had with him were two hand grenades, a rifle, one magazine of bullets, and three-quarters of a bottle of Jack Daniels whiskey. He heard the enemy chattering in German all around him and he was scared. He thought he was a goner. So Daddy chugged down that bottle of whiskey, and then he lobbed those two grenades. When he heard the second one explode, he stood up, spun around, and unleashed that whole magazine of bullets and killed every enemy soldier in sight on that beach!"

"Um, that's a very interesting story," the teacher said when I'd finished. "But what is the moral, Nino?"

"Well," I said, "the moral is: Don't mess with my daddy when he's drunk!"

Other than being called on in class, I loved school. It was a constant adventure.

14

Most of my elementary school teachers were dried-up spinsters. But not the young honey I had in fifth grade. Legs up to her ears, breasts round and full, thick blond hair flowing down her back: She was *schweet!*

Well, one day she was writing something high up on the blackboard and all the boys started giggling. She turned around and said, "Who's giggling?"

"It was me," replied this little boy in the front row.

"Well, what are you giggling about?"

"I was giggling," he answered, "because when you reach up high like that I can see your sweet thighs!"

"That's outrageous!" she said. "You're suspended for three days! Go to the principal's office immediately!"

A day or two later, the windows were open and it got chilly. The teacher grabbed that long pole used to close the upper part of the window. As she stretched to reach the top part of the window, she heard snickers coming from behind her.

Turning back around she demanded, "Carl, what are you giggling about?"

Carl's face turned beet red. "When you reached up to close the window," he said, "I saw your underpants!"

The teacher's face turned crimson. "Carl," she said sternly, "you're suspended for ten days!"

A week later, when our hot young teacher walked into class, her bloodshot eyes and pained grimace made it obvious that she'd been out partying the night before and was left with one heck of a hangover. It was also obvious that she couldn't wait for our morning quiet time, since she called for it to commence an hour early. She brought out the milk and cookies, after which we put our heads down on our desks and closed our eyes.

But I didn't fall asleep. After a few minutes, I looked up to see that the teacher had fallen into a deep sleep. Her head was tilted back, her mouth was open, and best of all, her legs were spread wide apart. A microsecond later, I realized, to my amazement, my teacher wasn't wearing any underpants!

When she awoke, she was surprised to see me standing in front of her desk, giggling.

"Whatever are you so happy about, Nino?" she asked.

"Well, ma'am, while you were sleeping your legs were wide open. I guess *my* school days are over!"

As much as I loved school, I have to admit that I wasn't necessarily the world's greatest student. I gave it my all, at least now and then, but my attention had a tendency to wander.

During one especially cold winter, the school custodian kept turning up the heat so high that every afternoon I'd fall asleep. One time Mrs. Belsky, the social science teacher, caught me napping. "Nino Mannelli," she said in a loud voice, "you can't sleep in my class!"

"Oh yes I could," I said, "if you'd keep your voice down a bit!"

The truth is, my interest in sex always overrode my interest in school.

Call it genetics. Call it environment. Call it innate curiosity. I have been interested in sex from almost the moment I popped out of Momma's womb.

I recollect being taught how to play doctor by a girl when I was no more than four years old. I suppose all kids go through that stage of exploration, but most of my buddies say they didn't even think about girls until they were around ten, eleven years old. Not me!

So there we were, this cute little girl and me—naked

behind the garage. Momma caught us just as my friend was in the midst of conducting a rather thorough physical exam.

"What the hell is going on here, Nino?" Momma yelled.

"We're just playing doctor," I said, trying to pull my clothes back on.

"Doctor, indeed," she said, grabbing me by the ear. "Young lady, take your clothes and go home. And you, young man—come with me!"

Following Momma indoors, I grabbed my little britches and hopped into the house. I don't think I've ever seen her so mad. She went right to the phone and called the little girl's mother.

"This is Mrs. Oscar Mannelli," she said in an angry voice. "I'll have you know my little boy and your little girl were playing doctor behind the garage."

I could hear the woman through the receiver. "That's natural," she replied calmly. "Don't get so upset. All kids go through a discovery stage. That's why they play doctor!"

"Yes," I heard Momma say. "But your daughter was giving my son *liposuction!*"

A couple of years later, I was still in my "discovery stage" and was sitting in the backyard, wailing away. I was back behind the garage, going at it, when Daddy suddenly strolled around the corner and saw what I was doing. I was pretty embarrassed and a little scared, too. But he actually seemed pleased to see I was getting "acquainted" with my body.

"What are you doing, son?" he asked. There was a big old grin on Daddy's face.

"Why, I'm playing soldier," I explained. "But I just

couldn't get this private to stand at attention until I started giving him some serious persuasion. But look at him now!"

Daddy took a look and chuckled. "You better slow down," he said. "If your persuading gets any more serious, it'll soon be *mess* call!"

Further sexual development came in seventh grade when I was dancing with Becky Lou Buckholtzer at the Spring Sock Hop. The band started to play some slow music, and I held Becky Lou close enough to feel her beating heart, close enough to feel her ta-tas pressed against my chest. As we swirled around the dance floor, I was struck by an idea.

"Becky Lou," I whispered in her ear, "we've been going out a while and, well, I was wondering—would you mind if I copped a feel?"

She looked at me aghast and said, "Good heavens, Nino!"

"I apologize if I'm being too forward," I replied, "but we've been going out for quite awhile now, Becky Lou, and I really do like you and . . ."

"Well," she said sweetly, "I understand. Go ahead."

With her permission, I reached down and squeezed my doodads!

By the time I graduated from elementary school, I'd already developed a philosophy on life and the pursuit of ta-tas and ingus. I believed then, as I believe now, that to get things to come to you, you have to act like you don't need anything at all. I think this probably was instilled in me the night my parents went to visit some friends in New Jersey and hired a baby-sitter to watch over my baby sister, Nadine, and me.

Momma and Daddy had barely pulled out of the driveway when the baby-sitter asked me if I would like to play a game of Monopoly with her. "Sure," I said, with a well-practiced shrug of indifference.

I gave her the same blasé answer when, only moments later, she asked if I'd like to sit next to her on the couch. Nadine was safely tucked away and asleep, and so there we were: Me, not more than twelve years old, wearing my jammies; and the baby-sitter, a nineteen-year-old college student, picking up some extra dough, sitting side-by-side on the couch. Her perfume was intoxicating. She rubbed my back and I rubbed hers. We stole a kiss, then a hug, and then a squeeze. I was in bliss. Her ta-tas were sweet akimbo! Oh God, I'm getting ten-hut at the memory of it.

I was so into what we were doing that I didn't hear the key in the front door lock. You can imagine my shock and horror when I heard Momma's voice say, "Oh my God, Oscar, look at Nino!"

I turned my head and there were my parents, standing in the front hall in disbelief. While they were busily collecting their thoughts, I disentangled myself from the baby-sitter and stood up. "Hey," I said with a big smile, "there's no reason to be upset because there's a real upside to this situation."

"Oh, yeah?" Daddy said. "And what would that be?"

"Well," I explained, "you won't have to pay the baby-sitter anymore. She's taking it out in *trade!!*"

I couldn't keep my mind off sex, even in church. Although I don't attend church regularly now, it was a Sunday ritual at the Mannelli house when I was growing up. Nadine and I would always try to sleep late—and Daddy would always yank us out of bed. Then the four of us would set off for church together, with Daddy occasionally slapping us in the back of our heads, as we walked down the street in our ill-fitting, Sunday-come-to-meeting outfits.

Every Sunday, rain or shine, Nadine and me would be front and center listening to the pastor spill his guts. The man could really get into that fire and brimstone stuff. I'll never forget the time he was banging the pulpit, ranting about sex.

"Sex!" he shouted. "That's all Americans think about! That's all they talk about! Sex! Sex! SEX! It's an outrage! You see it in all the magazine advertisements! You see it on television! It's used to sell everything from cigarettes to automobiles! Sex is permeating our very existence!"

The good pastor paused a second to catch his breath. In a much calmer voice, he continued. "Not that there's anything wrong with sex. Sex is a communication between two very special people in a very special marital situation. But people who talk about it or do it all day long . . .

"Well," he said, his voice getting louder and angrier again, "let me tell you something: *Sex is not going to pay the bills!*"

It was at that point in the sermon that Daddy jumped to his feet. "Oh yeah?" he yelled. "Why don't you go down and talk to Madam Lucy at the cathouse—she'll tell you all about bill paying!"

Momma thought it was good for me to occasionally accompany the pastor on his rounds when he visited the elderly, or the infirm. A lot of people thought he only worked on Sundays, but that was not the case. He worked all week long, visiting people in trouble and in need. I'd carry his bag as he went on his rounds.

One afternoon we visited an old man who was on his deathbed. The pastor stood at the end of the bed and prayed for the old man's soul.

"Cast out the devil! Deny him! Call the devil what he is: evil, awful, abominable! Denounce him with your last breath."

Through it all, though, the old man just laid there looking at the ceiling. Eventually, the pastor got frustrated. "You're near death," he said to the old man. "Why not leave this earth in peace? Denounce the devil!"

The old guy shifted his gaze from the ceiling to the pastor. "To be honest, Pastor," he said, "until I know for certain which way I'm headed, I don't want to aggravate *anybody!*"

Sometimes I wonder which way *I'm* headed.

Lord knows I've tried to lead my life down a straight and narrow path, but it's been difficult. Life has corrupted me.

One time my childhood buddy Tony Calachecci and I were walking down the streets of the Grand Concourse in our Bronx neighborhood when we found a discarded love sheath.

We were eight years old and not at all familiar with condoms. I held it between my thumb and forefinger and examined it. "Tony," I said, "do you know what this is?"

"No, Nino, I've never seen one of those before."

I had an idea. "Let's take it over to the drugstore and see if Mr. Robertson can figure out what it is."

So off we went to the local pharmacy. I held it up in front of the druggist. "Do you know what this is, Mr. Robertson?" I asked. "We found it in an alley."

He studied it for a minute or two. Evidently deciding

not to pollute our young, virgin minds, he finally said, "Oh, that's a cow's teat. They're shedding them this time of year."

With that bit of newly acquired knowledge neatly tucked in our eight-year-old brains, Tony and I left the drugstore, and began walking back home. We'd walked a block or two when Tony said, "Well, Nino, what do you want to do with it?"

"I guess we better just throw it away." I sighed. "Hell, we could have sold it if we hadn't sucked all the milk out of it!"

CALLER: *Grease, I'm having no luck with the women— what should I do?*

GREASEMAN: *You might want to try expanding your demographics. As Daddy used to say: Women are like dog turds—the older they get, the easier they are to pick up!*

Chapter 2

My Daddy

Oscar Grease Mannelli. My daddy. He's the reason we had to reinforce the chandelier with heavy-duty toggles and bolts in the ceiling. He's the reason we have to notify the police if we're having a party so they don't come down and bust it up. He gets so rambunctious it's a wonder he hasn't been locked away for a hundred years by now. If your heart has gone out to Joey Buttafuoco's wife, Mary Jo, think about what my mother has had to put up with all these years.

And after reading a bit about Daddy, you'll have a pretty good idea how I ended up the way I am.

I remember the time Momma walked into the house and caught Daddy in the throes of passion with some hussy. Momma stood there, hands on her hips, tapping one foot on the floor. "You're a vile man, Oscar Grease Mannelli! You disgust me! Bringing this hussy into our own house, having your way with her on our couch where we watch TV night after night!"

And They Ask Me Why I Drink?

At that point the woman spoke up.

"Now, now, Mrs. Mannelli," she cooed, "don't you blame old Oscar. After all, he wouldn't need a girlfriend if you'd give him enough allowance money to pick up a hooker every now and then!"

Then there was the occasion Momma had her sewing circle ladies over for lunch. Daddy was running around the kitchen, pinching and slapping the women's butts. These were all fine, upstanding women, pillars of the community, not the sort of women Daddy was used to carousing with. One woman looked him straight in the eye and said, "Oscar Grease Mannelli, would you please act your age!"

I happened to be passing through the kitchen just as she admonished him, and I was horrified at what she'd said. After Daddy stormed out of the room, I turned to the lady. "You shouldn't have said that," I said.

"Really?" she smugly replied. "And why not?"

"Well, you see," I replied rather sheepishly, "Daddy turned sixty-nine today!"

One morning Daddy was hung over, and he was just sitting at the kitchen table, staring off into space, drinking his coffee and smoking his Tipparillo. Momma stood across the table glaring at him. Finally unable to ignore her stare, he looked up and said, "What are you glaring at, woman? I didn't make any noise when I came to bed last night!"

"That's true," she sneered. "But the four guys that dragged you in sure did!"

When I got to be around thirteen years old, Daddy began taking me down to Miss Lucy's every week. She ran the best cathouse in town. One Saturday night we went down there, and it was sheer pandemonium. There were couples hobbling and gobbling in the backyard. There were couples having ingus in the front yard. There was a guy getting a snarlin' on the lawn near the bus stop. In fact, everywhere I looked there were sweating bodies. Why, they were even doing the Flying Gamahooch, hanging from the limbs of trees in the backyard!

Stepping over and around all the bodies, we finally managed to get up to the front porch of Miss Lucy's. Daddy pounded on the door and when Miss Lucy opened it, he said, "Miss Lucy, what the hell is going on here?"

"Are you blind, Oscar? Can't you see? We're having a yard sale!"

Coming home from Miss Lucy's another night, Daddy and I found Grandma Mannelli, poor old senile soul, in the kitchen using the broom handle like it was a vibrator.

Well, it was a pretty disgusting sight. But what was really weird was that she had placed a condom over the end of the broom! Not knowing exactly what to do, we both laughed. Daddy said, "Granny, what are you doing with that condom on the end of that broom? You know you can't get pregnant from a broom handle!"

"Pregnant?" Granny cackled. "I ain't worried about getting pregnant. I'm worried about getting *splinters!*"

I remember the time Daddy got his hands on four Redskins' tickets. This was quite a coup, because those games sell out years in advance. Daddy told Momma he was going to take two of his buddies and me to see the game. But there were no buddies, unless you count two luscious hussies as buddies.

We had great seats, right on the fifty-yard line, but

And They Ask Me Why I Drink?

Daddy wasn't paying any attention to the game. He was too busy messing with the women. He was kissing them, pinching them, tonguing them—all around loving 'em!

Finally I leaned over to him. "Daddy, you'd better be careful or we're going to wind up in a whole heap of trouble!"

Of course, he didn't listen to me.

A few minutes later, just as Daddy had a lip lock on one of the girls, the guy who dresses up like an Indian at all the Redskin games started doing his Indian dance right in front of us. He was in full Indian regalia, from headdress to moccasins.

Naturally, the minute he started beating his tom-tom and dancing, the TV cameras zoomed in on him. And who do you think was filmed right along with the Indian? That's right—Daddy! Right in the midst of tonguing this wench, Daddy looked up and saw the cameras on him. He realized that Momma, who was home watching the game, had probably seen everything. We stayed for the rest of the game, but all the way home Daddy was talking to himself, trying to figure out what to say to Momma. When we got home, Daddy jumped out of the car and hotfooted through the front door. And he never stopped talking from the minute he got inside.

"Hi hon, boy oh boy, was that a heck of a game! Not only that, but guess what? I ran into my twin brother there! Yeah! I thought he'd been shot in Korea years ago. But, no! He just dropped out of sight for a while. He was at the game, with some sleazebag, tonguing her all through the game. It was disgusting. Me and the guys were making fun of them . . . Ha ha ha ha . . ."

Momma just stared at him as he went through his monologue. Then, when he'd run out of conversation, she said, "Hell, isn't that something, Oscar! What a coincidence! You run into your missing twin brother and he's kissing some sleazebag. At the very same moment, I ran into my long-lost twin sister. She was giving our next-door neighbor a snarlin'!"

Despite all of my wild tales about life with Daddy, the truth is that he was the most instrumental person in my development, and was almost single-handedly responsible for making me the man I am today. Virtually ever turning point in my life was either created or witnessed by Daddy. Nowadays people think nothing about discussing sex, incest—you name it. In fact, I don't believe there's a taboo left that hasn't been examined on one of those TV talk shows. But when I was growing up, nobody ever talked openly about those subjects, and maybe not even in the privacy of their own homes. Nobody, that is, except my daddy.

Sex was one of his favorite topics, which probably explains why he knew so much about it. He never tired of discussing the mysteries surrounding the male-female mystique. Put quite simply, Daddy was truly a man ahead of his time.

I think I was in my early teens when I first began wondering who I really was as a person, and at the time I was seriously questioning my sexual identity. I went straight to Daddy with my confusion.

It was a Saturday afternoon and we were alone in the house. Momma had taken my sister, Nadine, to the beauty parlor for her very first permanent, and Daddy was sitting in his favorite chair, reading the newspaper. I went into the living room, and sat down on the couch across from him. "Daddy, don't get mad at me but . . . I think I might be a homosexual!"

Daddy's gaze jumped from the paper to me and he

practically swallowed his Tiparillo. He slammed down the sports section and stood up.

"So you think you may be one of those fudgepackers, huh?"

"Well," I said, "I'm just not sure. I have doubts about myself."

Daddy stared at me in silence for a moment, then said, "All right, let's just put you to the tailgater test!"

And with that, he dropped trou, grabbed that nodule-laden implement, and held it in front of me. "Okay, son," he said. "Does this look good to you?"

Before I could answer, he put it right in my face. "C'mon," he said. "Put it right under your nose like a good cigar. There," he said, holding that thing under my nose. "Does that smell good to you?"

I felt my stomach begin to churn and my throat start to constrict. Nausea was welling up inside me as Daddy said, "I'm going to put you to the real test!"

He spun around, dropped down on his hands and knees, and slid under the coffee table. "So," he bellowed, wiggling his big, ugly *tokhis* in my face. "How's this look to you? Does that look real romantic? Because that's what you're gonna be dealing with on a regular basis if you're gonna flip-flop and criss-cross on me!"

Daddy was still under the table talking as I raced across the room, threw open the patio door, and ran outside. I literally heaved my guts by the above-ground pool in the backyard. When I'd finished, Daddy came over and put a tattooed, muscular arm around me.

"I could never face anything like that," I told him.

"Well then," he said, "you ain't no homosexual."

He turned around and headed back to the house. "Now you run along," he said over his shoulder, "because your momma's back from the beauty shop with your sister.

My Daddy

Don't say anything to Momma," he added, "but yesterday Nadine told me she thought *she* was a *lesbian!*"

He heaved a big sigh. "I've got to hurry," he whispered, "because *Roseanne* is going to be here in about fifteen minutes to help me convince Nadine otherwise!"

I was proud to be Daddy's boy, the student who learned from the master. Perhaps the following tale will demonstrate just how much I was picking up from Daddy, even in my tender teenage years.

When I was about fifteen, one of our sweet Bronx girls turned up pregnant. Her father found out and invited all of us neighborhood boys over for a discussion. "I know my daughter's been frisky with a lot of you," he said, "but one of you went all the way and she won't tell me who. So I'm going to ask you myself. Which one of you put the stones to her?"

He looked around the living room, then began asking each of us the same question. "Buzz, was it you?" "No, sir, it wasn't me!" "Willie, were you the one stabbing her on a regular basis?" "No, sir. It wasn't me."

Finally he turned his attention my way. "Nino," he said, "you've never lied to me. Did you get my daughter pregnant?"

"Well, sir," I said, "to tell you the truth, I did not get your daughter pregnant. However, I *did* have a *hand* in it!"

Don't be too judgmental of Daddy and his wild and crazy ways. Yeah, he'd drink and run all over town and dally with the damsels, but I'd be by his side. At least we were together! That's more than I can say for a lot of fathers and youngsters growing up today.

I remember when I joined the Cub Scouts, we conned Daddy into becoming a reluctant scoutmaster. He hated wearing that little outfit and the scarf and everything, but he did it for me. He did it because I wanted to be in the Cub Scouts.

After taking us on a nature hike and to the museum and all the rest of the usual Cub Scout stuff, Daddy gathered the scouts together. "Boys," he said, "I've got something you're going to like. I don't think they have a Merit Badge for it, but it's going to be *schweet!*"

That was the first time Daddy took me—and the rest of the Cub Scouts—to Miss Lucy's cathouse. Miss Lucy herself, all perfumed and powdered, was waiting for us, surrounded by her legion of hussies. The lovely ladies were just sitting there, staring at us, a bunch of little boys.

Daddy just grinned. "Boys, prepare yourselves, because you're going to have your firsthand experience."

I was really disappointed to hear that.

"Psst, Daddy," I whispered. "I was sort of looking forward to a *slice.* I've already had my first *hand* experience!"

In his defense, I have to say that Daddy came by his excessive interest in sex naturally, part of his legacy from his own father, my Grandpa. In truth, Grandpa never did lose his keen regard for the opposite sex, even in his more advanced years.

One night, when I was all grown-up and Grandpa was idling his time in an old-age home, I got a phone call from Grandpa's nurse. The nurse told me that the home wanted Grandpa Grease out. If he didn't leave of his own accord, she said, they would throw him out.

Naturally, I raced right over and went directly to the manager. "What's the problem?" I asked.

"The problem," the fellow said, "is that your grandfather is making a terrible ruckus about his room. He says his room is dangerous and he demands to move. But we don't have any other rooms available. Besides, all of the rooms are identical! So he's got to go."

"All right," I said, "calm down, sir, calm down. Let me go up and see what I can do with Grandpa."

So I hotfooted it up to Grandpa Grease's room. "What's all this commotion about your room? What do you mean it's dangerous? It looks like everybody else's room."

"No, it isn't. Come here!"

I followed him over to the window. "Do you see that window across the alleyway?" he said. "Do you see that girl in there? Well, she gets undressed in front of that window every night, and as nearsighted as I am, I've got to lean way out the window to get a good look. And if I lean out any farther, one of these nights I'm going to kill myself! That why I'm telling you: *this room is dangerous!*"

CALLER: *Grease, I just finished a book on the Donner party. How hideous! Can you ever imagine eating human flesh?*

GREASEMAN: *Well, I've had my share of scamper, of course. Scamper's best when served raw—and unlike bread, you don't want any crust.*

CALLER: *But what about flesh, Grease? What about that?*

GREASEMAN: *The only time I've had cooked flesh was with my buddy Moise Chumba, back in the deepest, darkest jungles of the Belgian Congo. We were mighty hungry and Chumba killed and cooked a local native boy. He started chomping on the top and I started at the bottom. Well, after a while, he asked if I was enjoying my meal. "I'm having a ball!" I replied. "Then you better slow down," he said. "You're eating too fast!"*

Chapter 3

Favorite Bedtime Stories

During my early, tender years, when I had trouble falling asleep, Daddy would come into my room and sit on the side of the bed. He would brush the hair out of my eyes and tell me a story. This was an entirely normal thing for parents to do—but Daddy's stories were anything but normal. One of them concerned a cannibal feast:

"Once upon a time there were these cannibals preparing to celebrate an upcoming cannibal holiday. Several
weeks before the celebration, they divided into groups to
travel far and wide to round up food for their holiday feast.

"On this particular holiday foray, the first thing they did
was capture a couple of missionaries. They dragged them
into the camp and threw them into a large pit for
safekeeping. Then another group returned with a big-
game hunter. They tied him up and tossed him into the pit
with the missionaries. A third cannibal contingent came
with an entire bus full of tourists and chucked them—
funny shirts, shorts and cameras included—into the pit."

The cannibals were so happy and excited that they
began to dance.

"Yeaaa," they shouted in cannibalese, jumping up and
down as they danced around a huge bonfire. "This is
going to be the biggest feast we've ever had!"

They were right in the middle of their precelebration
festivities when a small plane appeared on the horizon.
Minutes later, landing in a dusty clearing not far from the
cannibal's village.

The dancing stopped and everyone watched as a couple
of cannibals got out of the plane, pulling several people
clad in pajamas after them.

One of the missionaries down in the pit stood on the
shoulders of a fellow missionary so he could peer over the
top. Thoroughly puzzled by the scene, he signaled to
the cannibal chief.

"Excuse me," the missionary said in his best cannibalese, "but I'm curious. Who are those people in pajamas?"

A toothy grin spread across the chief's face. "This is a
very important holiday for us," he explained, "so I sent a
couple of our warriors by plane to a mental institution in

London. You see, when we have our feast we want everything . . . from soup to *nuts!"*

Another of Daddy's stories concerned an American baseball team that was traveling through Africa on an exhibition tour.

The team's chartered plane was flying over some uncharted region deep in the Congo when the wing caught fire. The plane crashed in the jungle. Miraculously, the baseball players survived, and almost all of the athletes hacked their way through vines and trees and swamps of the Congo back to civilization. Unfortunately, a couple of them got captured by cannibals.

When the triumphant warriors returned to camp with the captured players, the chief ordered a big fire built and announced there would be a great feast that night.

Later that night, these two cannibals were sitting around the fire, enjoying their dinner. The one cannibal said to the other, "So, what do you think of the right fielder?"

The other cannibal took a big bite of meat off the bone he was holding. "I don't think he's star material, but he's got a *great arm!"*

As a result of listening to all of Daddy's stories, the Congo—a land of mystery and danger, intrigue and lost souls, still unconquered—has held a special fascination for me my entire life. Even in this day and age you go there at your own risk, and confront the savage cannibals residing within its deep, dark rain forest.

At one point, I decided that I had to see this amazing place for myself, and off I went. I roamed everywhere, plunging into the rivers with the crocodiles and climbing high into the mountains with the gorillas. Miraculously, I made friends with the various cannibal tribes. In fact, I not only made friends, I was accepted as one of their own, (although I declined to indulge in their exotic fare).

One afternoon, I accompanied a father and his young son as the man taught the boy, who couldn't have been more than ten years old, how to track human prey. Wearing war paint and carrying their spears, the two silently slid through the jungle until they came upon a lagoon. A beautiful young woman was swimming in the crystal clear waters. She had tawny brown skin, full ripe lips, and a *tokhis* so round and tight you could have bounced a softball off it all day long.

"Breakfast!" the boy said to his father. "Let's sneak over, kill her, and eat her!"

After taking a long, lustful look at the young woman, the father shook his head. "Not exactly," he replied. "We will sneak over and capture her, son. But then we'll go home and kill and eat your *mother!*"

CALLER: *You're always talking about your daddy. How come you don't have any zesty stories about your momma?*

GREASEMAN: *That's 'cause I was the only hell my momma ever raised!*

Chapter 4

My Momma

Even though I'm going on and on about Daddy, I don't mean to shortchange Momma. After all, Momma held the family together, in spite of Daddy's sexual hijinks.

Still, she and Daddy fought like cats and dogs for years. When I got older, I got dragged into the fussin' and the feudin', because Momma would always try to find out what Daddy was up to by grilling me.

"Where's your father?" she'd ask. "I hear he's been unfaithful. Well, I'm going to find out with who and scratch her eyes out! Just wait 'til he gets home. I'm going to give him what fer!"

While I loved Momma with all my heart, it was my sacred duty as a son to protect Daddy. I snuck out the back door and ran down to Delancy's bar, where I knew he'd be.

"Daddy," I said breathlessly. "Momma's on the warpath! She knows you've been up to something and she's going to confront you when you get home!"

Daddy just grinned, but he got up from the bar, and the two of us started walking home. "Aren't you going to hide out somewhere?" I asked.

"Hell no," he said. "I'm just going to face it, son."

When we got home, I sat outside on the porch because I didn't want to hear the sound of glass shattering and bones breaking. And sure enough, the moment Daddy got inside I heard Momma confront him.

"Oscar Grease Mannelli!" she screamed. "Who have you been seeing? Don't lie to me! I know you've been seeing somebody and I want to know who!"

I heard Daddy say, "Oh yeah? Well, if you know so much, who do *you* think I'm seeing?"

"I think you're seeing Ethel Merriweather," she said. "Ever since her husband died, Ethel Merriweather's been a pushover. All the guys in town know Ethel's is where you go if you want a little action!"

Daddy chuckled. "I ain't seeing Ethel Merriweather!"

Momma shrieked. "Oh, no, Oscar, don't tell me you're seeing Lurleen Pickitt, the barmaid! Why, you put five dollars under your glass when you finish your drink and you get it in the parking lot. Don't tell me you're seeing that hussy!"

"No," Daddy calmly replied. "I ain't dating Lurleen Pickitt."

"Oh my God," Momma cried. "Then you're going out with Martha Pepperidge. Ever since she got divorced she's been taking out revenge on her husband by dating as many men as she can, giving them anything and everything they want! That's who you're seeing, isn't it? Martha Pepperidge!"

"No, I ain't seeing Martha Pepperidge, either."

"I'll find out who it is," Momma said, "and when I do

there's going to be big trouble, Oscar! You hear me? Big trouble!"

Daddy walked outside, lit a Tiparillo, and sat down on the porch next to me.

"Did Momma find out who you're hobbling?" I asked.

"Nope," Daddy said with a big, wide grin, "and not only that, son, I got me *three new leads!*"

The fighting and the tension continued. I finally convinced my parents to go to a marriage counselor by promising to go with them. Neither of them said a word as I drove them downtown for the appointment. Neither of them said anything after they'd gotten situated in the counselor's office, either.

So I talked for them and explained how they had drifted apart, and how they no longer seemed to share any of life's joys together. The counselor took notes and listened intently until I was finished.

"Well, Mrs. Mannelli," he said, "what you need to do is take a more active interest in Oscar's interests. I mean, if you start showing that *you* like what *he* likes, maybe you'll find a common ground."

"Hey," Momma snorted. "if I liked what he likes, I'd be a lesbian!"

Momma definitely had it tough with Daddy. Though I loved that man dearly, I can't say that he was always in the right.

For instance, I was standing nearby when Momma, pregnant with my sister, Nadine, called the doctor. "Doc," Momma said, "I got to ask you a question. You see, my husband wants to know . . ."

The doctor must have interrupted her because Momma fell silent for a moment. Then I heard her say, "No, Oscar didn't ask me about making love while I'm pregnant. He wants to know if I can still *cut the grass!*"

One time, Daddy took Momma to the hospital, because she was suffering from awful abdominal cramps. After examining her, the doctor told Daddy he was going to have to put Momma in the hospital.

"I'm sorry," the doctor said, "but she has some sort of intestinal blockage. She'll be in here at least a week."

I saw the look of panic flash across Daddy's face when he heard what the doctor had to say. And then I heard Daddy's response and I was appalled. Appalled!

"Well, Doc," Daddy said. "If you're going to take my wife away, can't you at least give me a *loaner?*"

Speaking of cramps reminds me of the time Momma went shopping and asked Daddy, who was watching a ball game, if he'd look after me. "Now you watch Nino," Momma said, "because the last time I went shopping and left you in charge, I came home and found him getting ready to gargle the Draino!"

"Don't worry," Daddy said. "I'll watch him. You go ahead with your shopping and have fun."

Momma left and Daddy continued watching the ball game. After four or five beers, he fell fast asleep. So I started rummaging around, looking for something to play with.

I strolled into the bathroom and found boxes of those feminine pads, with the adhesive backing on them, under the sink. There were tons of them, because Momma used to buy them by the case at her favorite discount store.

Bored, I transported those boxes into the bedroom and idly removed a handful of sanitary pads from the boxes. I unwrapped a couple and stuck them to the wall. For some reason, I became enthralled by the act of slamming those sticky sanitary napkins against the wall. In fact, I got so carried away I stood on the dresser and slammed 'em high up. Then I stood on the bed, stacked two chairs on top of each other, and slammed 'em two deep on the ceiling.

Hours passed and I could still hear Daddy snoring in front of the television. I suppose it was the sound of Momma's car pulling into the driveway that finally woke him. The next thing I knew, Momma was in the downstairs hall, and Daddy was standing in the bedroom door, looking slack-jawed at the decorating I'd accomplished during his nap.

Just then Momma walked up behind him. She peeked into the room from over his shoulder and began to scream, "Oscar! *Oscar!*"

Daddy reacted with lightning speed. "Calm down, dear," he said. "After all, you predicted this. How many times have you told me I'd end up in a *padded cell?*"

CALLER: *I'm zapping my best friend's sister, and I feel guilty about it. You see, he just died.*

GREASEMAN: *I know how you feel, and here's what you do: Wear a black condom out of respect for the dead.*

Chapter 5

My Sister Nadine

If I was a hellion growing up—and I surely was—my sister Nadine certainly ran a close second, especially as a teenager. I remember Daddy and Momma telling Nadine, "You know, you really need to go out on a date. You can't spend every Friday and Saturday night at home, using Nino's CB to talk to men over the radio. You need to see them face to face. We're going to fix you up with a date."

"Oh God no," Nadine screamed. "I don't want to date!"

"No," Momma persisted, "you're a grown-up young lady. You need to start going out on dates."

Momma started asking around the school, trying to find a nice boy who was also having trouble getting dates, thinking that two shy people could find a little happiness together. When she discovered that the head of the school debating team also hadn't been out on any dates, she phoned him and invited him over to meet Nadine—sight unseen.

And They Ask Me Why I Drink?

As it turned out, not checking him out was a big mistake.

About an hour before the fellow was to arrive, Momma and Daddy managed to get a reluctant Nadine to dress up and come downstairs. She was sitting on the couch, looking all nice and shiny in a pretty little chiffon dress, when Nadine's debating team champion came through the front door. He was one ugly looking guy: He had a beak of a nose, ravaged pock-marked skin, hideous teeth, and hair going every which way.

Nadine took one look at this wretched example of mankind standing in the living room and screamed, then jumped up and ran out of the room. You could hear her hollerin' all the way up the stairs to her room.

Excusing themselves, Momma and Daddy raced after her.

"All right," Daddy said, "so he's not a fancy fashion-plate model. But you need to be messing with some boys now. You're past the age of playing with dolls or Nino's CB radio. So you get in there and entertain that young man. He's waiting for you in the parlor. Now!"

Nadine trooped downstairs to the parlor. Daddy and Momma went downstairs, too, and I followed them into the den. As we passed by the parlor, however, we snuck a peek. It was obvious that the fellow was uncomfortable in his bow tie and his ill-fitting brown suit.

About a half hour later, I peeked into the parlor again. . . . I was shocked! Nadine was in there, face down, giving him a snarlin'!

I ran back to the den. "Momma! Daddy! Come look at this!" I whispered.

They followed me down the hall and peered into the room. The next thing I knew, Daddy went crashing in there, bellowing, "Good God, Nadine! You told me you didn't even like him!"

Nadine pulled her head out of the boy's lap, and wiped her mouth with the back of her hand. She looked up at Daddy and calmly said, "Anything to avoid looking at his *face!*"

That Nadine: she was always up to something. I remember being outside, washing the family car, when I saw Nadine walking up and down the block, pushing a baby carriage.

I stopped what I was doing and went over to her. When I got about six feet from her, I heard a baby crying. "Since when do you baby-sit?" I asked.

"Oh, leave me alone," she said and started pushing the carriage back up the sidewalk. I walked alongside her for a moment, then glanced in the carriage. Instead of a baby, a tape recorder was wrapped in a blanket!

"What in the blue blazes are you doing, Nadine?"

"Keep your voice down!" she said. "I'm trying to scare the hell out of a few guys I know!"

One time Nadine and I were having a snack in the kitchen, when we heard a strange noise coming from Momma's bedroom upstairs. It was a constant, whirring kind of noise. *Hmmmmmm . . . hmmmmmmm . . . hmmmm . . .*

Nadine looked at me. "What's that?" she asked.

"I don't know," I said. "Sounds like Momma's got an eggbeater in her bedroom."

Puzzled, we tiptoed up the stairs. I peeked through the keyhole and saw Momma lying on the bed, working this vibrator. She was churning up a serious lather!

And They Ask Me Why I Drink?

I told Nadine to go downstairs and fix us some cookies and milk. When she was safely away, I swung the bedroom door wide open. "Momma," I yelled. "What in the world is going on?"

Momma jumped straight up in the air. Then, regaining her composure, she said, "Relax, Nino, relax. I just wanted to make sure Nadine's birthday present wasn't *defective!*"

Speaking of presents, at Christmastime, Momma and Daddy, hoping for a little peace and quiet, would drop us off at Grandpa and Grandma's house. They loved having us visit, and we loved being there.

Nadine and I had twin beds in the guest room. Every night Nadine would get down on her hands and knees and start praying at the top of her lungs.

"Dear God," she'd begin, "I figure You know Santa Claus personally, because you're both big wheels, so would You mention my Christmas list to him? I mailed it to Santa, but he probably gets a million lists, so a word from You would mean so much. I've been so good this year, and I'd really like that bicycle. If You could arrange to have a basket attached to the handles that would be even better, because then I can carry around the Chatty Patty doll I'd also like and . . ."

Nadine was going on and on, and I finally couldn't take anymore. "Nadine," I said, "you don't have to pray so loud. God ain't deaf!"

Nadine turned around and winked at me. "I know—but Grandma is!"

I opted for a different tack with Santa, although, same as Nadine, I also got down on my hands and knees and prayed.

"Dear Santa," I said. "I would be ever so grateful if you would please bring me a red bicycle."

I thought about my appeal to the Jolly Fat Man all the next day, and decided I needed to be a little more forceful. That night, I changed my prayer. "Dear Santa," I said, "I've been a very good boy all year long, and really think I deserve a red bicycle."

That wasn't bad. Pondering the situation some more, though, I realized that if I wanted to get that bike, I better go all out. I stole into the living room and took down the framed picture of the Virgin Mary off the mantel. I placed it in a shoebox, put the lid on the box, and sealed it with duct tape. I hid the shoebox under my bed, and then got ready to pray. I decided to go over Santa's head, directly to the Big Guy.

"Dear Jesus," I said, "if You ever want to see Your Mother alive again, you'll tell that fat bastard Santa to bring me a shiny red bicycle, and pronto!"

CALLER: *How's the weight lifting going, Grease?*
GREASEMAN: *Great! My arms are huge.*
CALLER: *Is that the strongest part of your overdeveloped anatomy?*
GREASEMAN: *No. That would have to be my tongue.*
CALLER: *Your tongue?*
GREASEMAN: *Absolutely! My tongue: I can lift a 115-pound woman two feet off a bed with it!*

Chapter 6

Greek for a Day

Amazingly, despite my bizarre upbringing, I made it all the way through secondary school and got accepted into college. But before I could head off to this new adventure, I had to find myself a little transportation, a schweet ride to get me there.

Hence the purchase of my first car.

When it came to buying cars, new or used, Daddy was a master of negotiating, so he accompanied me to the dealer. On the way there, Daddy stopped in the red light district and, for seventy-five dollars, got a woman to come along to the car lot. I couldn't understand why we were bringing a hooker to buy a car.

"Never you mind, son," said Daddy. "Just play along with whatever I say and do."

A few minutes later, we pulled up to the lot. Daddy put

his arm around that luscious woman as we were walking to the office. Inside, I could see a guy in a plaid jacket, rubbing his hands together in anticipation of a sale.

"Can I help you, sir?" he asked Daddy.

"Yes," Daddy replied. "Me and the wife are looking for a car for our son. The boy needs some reliable transportation."

The guy looked across the lot and his eyes brightened. "I've got just the car for him," the salesman said. "Step right over here. This car is something your son will like, and your wife will rest easy knowing he has a safe, solid vehicle."

The next thing I knew we were sitting in the salesman's office, and he and Daddy were going back and forth on the price. Finally, the salesman got up to leave the room. "I've got to talk with the sales manager," he said over his shoulder.

A couple of minutes later he returned. "All right," he said. "This is the rock-bottom price we can give you."

Daddy looked at the price and tears welled in his eyes. "Let me confer with my family a second," he said soulfully, waving the salesman out of the room

Once he was gone, Daddy didn't say a word. He just sat there, silently smoking a Tiparillo. When the salesman returned, Daddy said, "Sir, I've discussed this with my wife, and if you'll knock another three hundred dollars off the price of the car, she'll give you a snarlin'."

"What?" the salesman said, dumbfounded.

Daddy sighed. "Look," he said, "this car is very important to us. I know you can cut the price down some. I promise you'll have the best snarlin' you've ever had in your life—but you gotta knock the price down three hundred dollars! Right, honey?"

The hooker nodded in agreement.

Shocked, the salesman said he had to speak to the sales manager about Daddy's counteroffer.

"Tell the sales manager there's a snarlin' in it for him, too!" Daddy yelled, as the guy raced out of the office.

Pretty soon the salesman and the sales manager came hotfooting down the hallway. "Are you sure about this?" they asked in unison.

"Well," Daddy said thoughtfully, "if you make it an even five hundred, we can get a snarlin' for the company president, too."

The two men looked at each other, then the sales manager said, "You've got yourself a done deal!"

The three of them disappeared into a backroom. Apparently, there was some mighty fine hobbling and gobbling, 'cause when it was over the guys were all smiles. Grinning, they stood in the lot and waved good-bye as we drove away in my new car.

Daddy was smiling, too. What a deal! A seventy-five-dollar hooker had saved him five hundred bucks. He was so full of himself, he just couldn't resist a final dig. As we drove past the salesmen, Daddy leaned out the window. "You all have been so nice to us, we're going to give you a little souvenir to remember us by."

The salesmen nodded and smiled. "That's nice," the manager said. "When can we look forward to it?"

"Oh," Daddy said, "you'll start to see signs of it in about three to ten days!"

My new wheels took me straight up to school. College was great! For the first time in my life, I was on my own. I felt free. I felt alive. I felt like my own person, ready and able to make my own decisions.

One of my first decisions was to join a fraternity. I was walking around campus, a puny, pencil-necked geek, proudly wearing my freshman beanie, when a guy from one of the more popular fraternities approached me. "Hey, Nino Mannelli," he said. "You're new on campus, aren't you?"

"Yes, sir," I said proudly. "I am."

"You don't have to call me sir," he said. "Matt Lebow's the name. I thought you might like to pledge my frat, I Felta Thi. We're having a big pledge party tomorrow night. Why don't you drop by?"

I accepted the invitation and went to the party. I was having a great time, too, drinking beer and listening to the guys' conversation. On my way for a second beer, Matt and another fellow came over to me. They told me it was time to play bingo.

"What do you mean 'bingo'?" I asked.

They laughed. "It's a little contest we hold," Matt explained. "A rite of manly passage during pledge week at I Felta Thi. There's really nothing to it. All the guys from the frat get in a room, turn out the lights, drop trou, and start wailing away. The first guy to achieve Shangri-la, the first guy to feel that bubbling masculine tide, yells, 'Bingo!' Then the rest of the guys gotta buy him beer, and wait on him hand and foot."

"Wow," I said. "Sounds a little spicy."

"It is," Matt said, "but we turn out the lights. So it's not as spicy as you might think."

"Okay," I said. "Let's play!"

They took me upstairs to a large bedroom, where I was determined to impress the upperclassmen with my manly prowess. As soon as the lights went out, I immediately started wailing. I was just going to town. My eyes rolled back in my head and I shouted, "Oh, God, yes! Yes! BINGO!"

The lights came on. Everybody else was completely

dressed! They'd even brought a couple of sorority girls into the room. There I was, caught in the spotlight, the butt of the joke, in all my naked nodular splendor. Everyone was pointing at me and laughing.

With tears of humiliation rolling down my cheeks and their laughter ringing in my ears, I managed to find my trousers and flee. Throughout my entire college career, my nickname was "Bingo."

If you don't believe me, look it up in the yearbook. You'll see my smiling duffus face, with "Bingo" underneath. Years later, it was with mixed emotions that I greeted the news that the school had launched a scholarship for promising young broadcasters. It was called the Bingo Fund.

During my sophomore year I met my very own Mrs. Robinson. She was a handsome woman—divorced, in her fifties—with a serious penchant for college boys. She frequented a bar near the fraternity, the better to eye the young flesh that gathered around.

A lot of the guys were reluctant to put the stones to her, but not me.

"Hey," I told them, "an old lemon may not give as much juice, but it still feels good when you squeeze it." With that I strolled on over to her barstool.

Over the course of the next couple of weeks, we shared a few drinks and a few laughs. Then, one night, she spilled her guts to me.

She had been really knocking back the bone-dry martinis, and something inside her snapped. She confided that even as far back as high school she had been attracted to younger men. All of her husbands—and there had been a handful—had been younger than she. But her troubles really began after her first husband left her for a young filly his own age.

Overexposure to the sun during her youth had taken its toll, and her skin had lost some of its elasticity. After her first husband left, she started thinking that perhaps her slowly sagging skin was the cause of her marital problems. So when she married again, she went straight to a plastic surgeon and made an appointment for a face-lift. Despite the lift, however, the second marriage failed in less than a year.

A couple of months after the divorce was final, the woman fell in love again, and immediately arranged for another face-lift. This third marriage also failed.

Upon meeting her fourth Mr. Right, she went under the knife again. No sooner had the bandages been removed from her face than her fourth husband filed for divorce. The day after the divorce was final, the woman, desperate, scheduled another appointment with the plastic surgeon. This time, however, he refused to operate. "I've given you four face-lifts already," he explained. "I can't do another one."

The woman was adamant. "Just one more," she begged. "I want to look my best. Just one more face-lift."

"Absolutely not," the doctor said. "It's not medically sound to perform so many face-lifts."

"Please," she cried, "I'm begging you, Doctor, don't turn me away. I'll never bother you again if you'll just give me one more face-lift."

Finally unable to withstand the woman's pitiful pleas, the doctor capitulated. The following week he performed the fifth face-lift.

After he had unwrapped the last bandage, the woman looked admiringly at her new countenance in the office mirror. "Hmmm," she said. "Looks good . . . but why did you put a dimple in my chin?"

"That dimple," replied the doctor, "is your navel! Let me give you a piece of advice: If you ever get another face-lift, you'll be *shaving!*"

I'll be honest with you: I wasn't the best student in the class. Still, I made decent grades, and I got through high school and college thanks to discipline and the knowledge that I was on my way to becoming a Boss Jock.

And I also got through thanks to the ultimate scam I learned during my four years of higher education. I couldn't wait to graduate so I could follow my dream. Now, as a public service, I am going to pass it on to you.

Sooner or later, there will come a time when, for whatever reason, you won't have a term paper ready when it's due. Not to worry!

First of all, make certain the term paper assignment is a really brutal complicated piece of work, and that it counts for half your grade. Then when the day comes to turn in the paper, don't turn anything in. Wait patiently until the day the teacher is due to return the grades, then jump into action!

Get to school early, run breathlessly into the classroom. "Professor, I know the class hasn't started yet, but I'm really anxious to get my grade on the term paper. You know how it is when you've worked hard on something and you feel like you've done well. Can you give me like a little hint on my grade? I mean, am I in the A range?—A minus? A plus?"

The professor will then look at you and exclaim, "Wait a minute. I never got a term paper from you."

The only proper response from you is "WHAT? I

worked six weeks on that paper! You didn't get it from me?!"

Next, turn around and smash your fist on the desk— whack! whack! whack! Begin to sob. "I busted my ass on that paper and you didn't get it! I don't believe you! What did you do with it?"

The professor will then begin to get upset. "I never got a term paper from you."

"You can put that on my tombstone!"

Put your fist through the window.

At this point the professor will try to calm you. *Remain hysterical.*

"Six weeks from morning to night working on that paper! I turn it in and you tell me you didn't get it!" Use your bleeding hand to bust the lock on the window. Open it up and stand out on the ledge. Begin shouting.

"This college career is going right out the window!"

The professor will undoubtedly jump up from his desk and rush toward you.

Scream: "I'm *jumping!* I'm going to flunk this course and you know what that means! I'll flunk out of school, get drafted, and get sent to Vietnam! I have nothing to live for!"

At that point, the professor will begin to cajole you. "There is more to life then a term paper. Come in here, we'll talk about it."

Maintain your ground. "No! I can't stand it! I'm going to jump!"

The professor will soon cave in. "All right! *All right!* Somehow your term paper must have gotten lost! I don't know how it happened, but it obviously did. Tell you what: You climb in the window, and I'll give you a B. How's that?"

Negotiate, "B plus. OR I'M JUMPING!"

CALLER: *I've got a friend here from Vietnam. He says he thinks you're his father.*

GREASEMAN: *Wow! That would be wild: one of my Vietnamese babies. Well, I did cut a lot of slices over there.*

CALLER: *He said his mother even named him after you.*

GREASEMAN: *Well, tell him I remember the exact last thing his mother ever said to me.*

CALLER: *What was that, Grease?*

GREASEMAN: *Twenty-five dollars!*

Chapter 7

Sergeant Fury

Every generation gets its chance to show its mettle. Mine did, back in the sixties, during the Vietnam War. I was in the Marines for two tours of duty over there. Those were the days when the name on my uniform said Grease Mannelli, but everybody knew me as *Sergeant Fury!*

Many people go through hell, but when it's over they put it behind them. They forget about it and get on with their lives. But Vietnam was something I will never forget. Since then, everything I do—waking to greet another sunrise, consuming a pile of Mallomars, taking a massive, watching a sports event, is a gift.

Every day I suck air is Christmas, because there was a

time when I didn't think I'd still be around to do so ever again.

I was a sniper in Nam. I volunteered for the position which requires tremendous patience and brains. I'd spend hours sitting in a tree, blending in with my surroundings, swaying with the branches, covered in the greenery and insects indigenous to the area. My rifle was always at the ready, waiting for the split second to make the perfect shot. With just a touch of my fingertip, another Viet Cong would go meet his ancestors.

I quickly became something of a legend. When I was with a unit and the rest of the guys were sleeping, I'd go out in search of the enemy. The guys would hear *kaboom!* in the middle of catching some shut-eye. Knowing Grease Mannelli had plugged another VC, they'd take off their helmets in respect.

A *Stars and Stripes* reporter came out to see me and asked, "What's your technique, Mannelli? You're up to a record 972 kills, practically the population of a small city! How did you get so many VC?"

"One of two ways," I confided. "Either way, you have to have the patience to wait and catch them at their most vulnerable moments. I've found the enemy is most vulnerable when he's making love. So, I'll sit in a tree with a view to the window of a hooch, and I'll wait until he's, uh, in position. Then I let him eat lead.

"The only other time a man is that vulnerable," I continued, "is when he's taking a massive out in a field somewhere. With just his head sticking up above the elephant grass, he's a perfect target."

When the article appeared, the headline immediately caught my attention. It read: "The Most Successful Sniper in the History of the American Military."

And They Ask Me Why I Drink?

I thought the reporter captured my *modus operandi* quite well. "Grease Mannelli," he wrote, "performs under a singularly simple motto: 'Always get them when they're coming or going!'"

One night we were camped outside a small Vietnamese village, trying to get some sleep before we moved into the DMZ. Unfortunately, everyone's stomach was rumbling because we'd had nothing to eat but government-issue slop for more than a week. On top of that, the sound of the villagers singing filled the night.

"I bet they're having a regular shindig," Robinson said to me as I sat by the fire, cleaning my rifle.

"Yeah," I said. "They're having a shindig and all I've got to eat is this can of fruits and peaches in heavy sauce. Man, I'd like a steak. I want some meat!"

"That's an affirm on that, sir," Robinson laughed. "I could sure go for some meat, too."

I stood up. "Robinson, DeLorenzo, Shapiro, Gallacheck," I said. "Come with me."

We walked to where the villagers had a water buffalo penned up. "Look at the size of that monster," I exclaimed. "I've heard of people eating them, you know. What do you think? There ain't nobody around."

Next thing you know, we had that big old water buffalo on a spit, over an open fire. "Hey," I said, giving the sizzling buffalo another turn, "while we're cooking this, why don't you guys go over to the village chicken coop and torch off some fried chicken?"

We cooked up one hell of a meal. Just as we were cutting into those juicy steaks, though, the lieutenant appeared. "What is the meaning of this?" he yelled. "These people rely on that water buffalo to plow their stinking fields. They rely on those chickens for sustenance. We are here to serve these people, not rape and pillage our way across South Vietnam. You will return all those steaks to the village and you will apologize. You will be docked three weeks pay, and you will pay for a new water buffalo! Do you read me loud and clear, Fury? *You will eat nothing that belongs to the villagers! You will eat what you've been issued, and that is it!*"

It was a melancholy moment as the men gathered up all the steaks and the fried chicken, and delivered them back to the villagers. Before turning in, I made my usual final check of the perimeter.

I was on my way back to my tent when I heard a strange noise coming from one of the hooches. I snuck over and peeked in. To my amazement, there was the lieutenant with one of the village girls. He was so busy giving a snarlin' that he didn't see me standing in the doorway until I finally spoke up.

"Excuse me, Lieutenant," I said. "But, aren't we violating our own ordinance here?!"

After my two tours of duty in Nam, I was sent home.

But while you can leave Nam, Nam never really leaves you. At one point, the shakes and the nightmares became so frequent I went to a VA Hospital to talk to one of the psychiatrists.

He wanted to know just how bad it had been in Nam. I took off my shirt and showed him where I'd gotten stitched up the back by a Viet Cong machine gunner. Then I pulled down my pants and showed him the shrapnel scars in my *tokhis*. I kicked off my shoes and showed him the hole in my foot.

"My God," he cried when I'd finished. "It's a wonder you're alive!"

And They Ask Me Why I Drink?

"It was hell. The only rest I ever got all those years was in Hawaii . . ."

And then I flashed back to 1967, when I was sent to Hawaii for some R & R. In those days, Honolulu was wide open—it was number one boom boom everywhere. You didn't even have to rent a motel to get a little ingus. Guys were getting snarlin's in the taxis from the airport. It was unbelievable! In the hotel you could rent a honey for the whole day.

I spent two weeks in Honolulu, and not a day went by that didn't see me double or triple deucing. I went from massage parlor to massage parlor, and I was up all night long.

By the time my two-week furlough was up, I flew back to Nam looking like hell. I had dropped twelve pounds. My eyes were bloodshot and I hadn't shaved once. I was all hobbled out.

"Mannelli," the lieutenant barked, "you're a pitiful excuse for a soldier! Fall in! Inspection in two minutes!"

I figured I was in deep trouble because the general was reviewing the troops. Sure enough, he stopped right in front of me.

"Sergeant," he said, "you look like hell!"

"I'm sorry, sir," I replied. "I've been in Nam a long time."

"Well, it shows!" he shouted. "You need some R & R, soldier! It's two weeks in Hawaii for you!"

More than one woman has commented on a tattoo adorning my hydraulics. Without fail, they squint and then ask, "What the hell is that?"

"They're sergeant stripes," I invariably say. "A legacy of my career in the armed services."

"Why sergeant stripes?"

"Because," I reply, "every now and then, *I like to pull rank!*"

CALLER: *Grease, my company is transferring me to West Virginia. Have any advice for me?*
GREASEMAN: *Yeah. Sleep on your back.*

Chapter 8

My Backwoods Summer Vacation

After my discharge from the army, I decided I needed a break from the hustle and bustle of modern life. Accordingly, I moved in with a country family in the hills of Appalachia. I spent several months in the backwoods of West Virginia, where the people were barefoot innocents and, well, kind of *tilted,* if you get my drift.

I should have known what I was up against. The Bronx school system had an exchange program with the West Virginia school system. When I was a high school junior, a fifteen-year-old girl from South Pawpaw came and stayed with us for several unforgettable weeks. The girl had an obsession with the bathroom.

At first, I thought she was spending so much time in there because she was entranced with the indoor plumbing and the running water. As the days went by, however, she began spending more and more time in the bathroom. Every night she'd get up after dinner, and spend an hour in the bathroom.

Finally, I sat her down and just came right out with it. "Do you have a bladder problem?"

"No," she said. "I don't have a bladder problem."

"Do you have a bowel blockage?"

She looked at me with disgust. "No," she replied. "I ain't got no bowel blockage."

"If there's nothing wrong with you," I said with exasperation, "what are you doing in the bathroom every night for an hour?"

"My momma told me when I came to live in the big city I should put on a clean pair of underwear every day. I've been here two weeks."

"I don't understand," I said. "What does that have to do with all the time you're spending in the bathroom?"

"Do you have any idea," she said angrily, "how long it takes to pull down fourteen pairs of underwear?"

I'll never forget my first trip to town during my Appalachian sojourn. I was walking along, window-shopping, when I glanced in one window and saw a man reach into a fishbowl and grab a goldfish. As I watched, he held the fish with one hand and began wailing with the other. Peering closer, I saw a woman in the back of the store running a lawn mower across the carpet.

As I was standing there, scratching my head at this bizarre sight, the sheriff came walking by. "Man alive!" I said to him. "You've got some real lunatics in this town!"

He stopped dead in his tracks. "What're you talking about?"

I pointed to the window. "Just look at this guy! He's got a fish in one hand and he's wailing with the other! And what about the woman in the back—she's rolling the lawn mower over the carpet!"

The sheriff just smiled. "You're new in town, ain't you

there stranger? These people are deaf. She's telling him to cut the grass and he's saying, 'Screw you. I'm going fishing!' "

The family I was staying with took in a blind girl. Despite her visual challenge, she was given the daily chore of milking the cows. This was of special interest to me, since I relied on the cow's milk for my morning coffee and corn flakes.

The blind girl would feel her way from the house to the barn, and give those cows a series of milk-yielding tugs on their swollen ta-tas.

One morning she returned from the barn, set down her bucket of milk, and sat down at the kitchen table just as I was getting ready to eat breakfast. I'd cooked some French toast, and was up for a glass of fresh milk. After pouring myself a glass, I took a big swallow . . . Agghhh!

A horrible taste flooded my mouth and I involuntarily spit the milk on the floor. I angrily looked at the blind girl. She was just sitting there, stabbing at the French toast and missing it.

"You stupid girl!" I screamed. *"You wailed away the bull again!"*

I was only in West Virginia for a few months but man oh man, did I leave there with a bunch of stories. If you've ever spent any time in West Virginia, you'll understand perfectly why it's pretty hard to separate fact from fiction.

Take the story I heard from this nurse I dated during my West Virginia repose. She worked the night shift in the emergency room at the General Hospital in Wheeling, so I used to meet her for breakfast at a little coffee shop not far from the hospital. One morning she came in, laughing herself silly.

It seems she had gotten a frantic call from a man whose wife was about to give birth, and the conversation had gone like this:

"Hello, Emergency? My wife's pregnant, and I think she's fixing to have the baby right now! Send the doctor!!"

"Has she broken her water?"

"Yes, she just broke her water! Send the doctor!"

"Is she having contractions?"

"Yes, she's having contractions—big time! Send the doctor!"

"Is this her first child?"

"No, dammit, this is her *husband!*"

Another time I was in the local tavern when a big, fat, good old boy strolled through the door. He yelled out, "The drinks are on me! Whatever you want!"

The bartender gladly served up a round of drinks. "What are you so happy about?" he asked the big spender.

"I came home early from work today, and caught my wife in bed with three guys!"

The bartender looked at the guy in disbelief. "Finding your wife in bed with three guys makes you *happy?!*"

"Sure," said the guy. "When I asked her what in the hell was going on, she told me, 'Oh honey, no one man could ever take your place!'"

Driving home that very same night, I saw the sheriff bent over a fellow who was sprawled on the sidewalk in front of the town's other bar. He looked like he could use some help, so I stopped. As I walked over to him, I heard the sheriff say, "Buddy, you've had enough to drink. It's time you headed home."

He yanked the guy to his feet and gave him a punch with

the back of his nightstick. The guy fell flat on his face again.

The sheriff yanked this fellow to his feet three more times—but each time the guy would just topple over.

"He's had way too much to drink," the sheriff said. "I'm going to have to drive him home. Will you help me get him into the patrol car?"

"No problem," I said. "In fact, if you want, I'll come along and help you get him out of the car too."

"I'm much obliged," the sheriff replied.

He looked in the guy's wallet and found his name and address. Together, we hauled the guy to the patrol car and dumped him in the back seat. Arriving at his house, we carried him to the front porch.

The house was dark. The sheriff beat his nightstick on the door until a woman in curlers and a robe finally appeared.

"Is this your husband?" the sheriff asked, stepping aside so she could see the unconscious man's face.

"Why, yes," she replied, "that is my husband . . . but where's his wheelchair?"

I was in the Pawpaw General Store one afternoon, when one of the young clerks said to the other, "Did I ever tell you I'm clairvoyant? That I know what people are going to say and do in advance?"

"In that case," the other boy said, "tell me what the next person who walks in here is going to ask for."

A couple of minutes later a woman walked in. She approached the counter, but before she could even open her mouth, the boy said, "Ma'am, I know why you're here. You're here to buy some Tampons!"

"No," the woman replied. "Actually I'm here to buy some toilet paper!!"

The boy looked at his buddy. "Hey." He shrugged. "I only missed it by t-h-i-s much!"

One of the big pastimes in West Virginia is hunting. All year long the men hunt. Some do it for sport; others do it to put fresh meat on the table. These three good old boys went hunting early one morning, and they got lost. By dusk they were hungry and tired. "What are we going to do, Jethro?" one of them asked. "No doubt about it, we're lost!"

"We've got to remember what we learned at Hunters' Safety School," Jethro replied. "If you're lost, fire a shot straight into the air so rescuers can track you down."

With that, Jethro fired through the trees straight into the air. Then he and his buddies sat down on a log and waited. After about fifteen minutes, one of the fellows said, "Jethro, I think you'd better fire another one!"

Jethro fired again. The three waited another half hour, but no one came to rescue them.

After another hour had passed and still there was no sign of help, Jethro stood up and exclaimed, "Jeez, I sure hope they find us soon! I'm getting cold, it's getting dark—and I'm almost out of *arrows!*"

I also got to do my share of hunting in West Virginia. There's nothing I like better than standing in the woods, waiting for the sun to come up, drinking a steaming cup of coffee with a bunch of guys, all prepared to blast Bambi at dawn's first early light. It's a great feeling. It's American!

One time I was lumbering through a treacherous swamp in the middle of nowhere when I heard a faint cry for help. I followed the sound for quite a distance until I came upon a black bog. A man was up to his chest deep in the middle of the deadly muck.

"Hang on, buddy!" I yelled.

He was sinking rapidly and his arms were outstretched toward me. I reached into my knapsack and pulled out a length of rope. I quickly made a lasso and tossed it out to him.

"Here," I shouted, "put that under your arms!"

He pulled the rope over his head and under his arms. I started pulling. Still, no matter how hard I tugged on that rope, he just kept sinking.

I couldn't believe it. All those years, working out in the gym—wasted!

In desperation, I wrapped the rope around a nearby tree, trying to gain some leverage. Once again, I pulled as hard as I could. But the guy kept sinking further into the mire.

I tied the rope around the tree and I took off running, yelling, "Help! Help! *Somebody help!*"

A couple of hunters heard my screams and came charging through the woods. "What's wrong?" they yelled.

I led the two of them back to the bog. The guy had continued to sink!

"Quick," I yelled to the hunters. "Grab the rope and pull! For the love of God, *pull!*"

The three of us began tugging on that rope with all our might. I could actually feel discs herniating in my back, but the guy still didn't budge. He just kept sinking.

Sweat was pouring down our bodies. It was unbelievable, impossible, that the three of us couldn't haul this guy out of that mire.

Just when I'd begun to give up any hope of rescuing

him, the guy yelled out. "Hey!" he called. "Do you think it would help if I took my feet out of the *stirrups?!*"

Another trip found me in a two-man deer stand with Bubba, a hunting buddy of mine.

Bubba and I were sitting in the stand, waiting for a deer to come along, when he whispered, "Hey, you know my son turned ten years old this weekend."

"Wow, that's unbelievable!" I said. "Seems like it was just yesterday that your wife, Rhonda, and I were going to the movies."

"Oh yeah," Bubba said, "I'd forgotten you and Rhonda used to date."

"Yeah, we did," I said, "but it wasn't any big thing, Bubba. Not like *you* and Rhonda. I mean, you two are married, with a ten-year-old kid."

Bubba was silent for a moment, then he said, "Uh, tell me the truth, Grease. Did you and Rhonda ever do, er . . . the nasty?"

"Aw, c'mon, Bubba," I replied. "It was a long time ago."

"I know. I'm just curious. I've always wondered about that. You're the one who brought it up that you used to date her. And whenever you're over for dinner, I wonder if Rhonda is looking at you with memories."

I laughed. "Rhonda and I had a nice time, but that was before you came into the picture. I think we'd just better drop it."

I was still laughing when Bubba swung his gun around and aimed it at my head.

"Don't point that at me," I said. "It's liable to go off!"

Bubba wasn't listening. "I'll drop you like a sack of potatoes," he said. His eyes narrowed into slits.

I heard the menace in his voice and saw his finger

tighten on the trigger. I jumped out of the stand just as he fired.

Bubba jumped out of the stand after me, screaming, "Did you nail Rhonda?"

I was running so fast through the woods, I couldn't see where I was going. I stumbled over a branch and fell face-down in the mud. Bubba came up behind me and flipped me over on my back.

"All right!" he said. "Before you die, you're gonna tell me just how you knocked the bottom out of my wife, Rhonda!"

"Wait a minute, wait a minute, Bubba," I cried. "I got a confession to make. One time we did get naked together. We were going to have us a little bit of ingus, but Rhonda was so beautiful that I couldn't do it. It was so humiliating . . ."

Bubba looked at me suspiciously, the barrel of his gun still aimed at my head. "So nothing ever happened?"

"No! She's one of those perfect women. I was so excited that I just couldn't do anything!"

A look of relief flooded Bubba's face. "Well, okay!" he said. He set his gun down and offered me a hand getting up.

"Of course," I added, once I was back on my feet, "it *did* take me a week to get that *shine* off my face!"

There was always something going down in West Virginia. I remember a story that made the front page of the local newspaper, which laid out the details of a big adultery trial held at the county courthouse.

To gain a conviction against the husband, the wife's attorney dispatched a private investigator to fetch the backwoods girl who was at the center of the case, to bring her into town for the trial.

According to the newspaper, the only way the PI could reach her was to paddle a canoe more than a dozen miles upstream, then hike for two days through heavy forest to her isolated cabin. Despite the difficult three-day journey, he managed to get there and back, girl in tow.

The courtroom was filled with excitement as the girl, barefoot, beautiful, and innocent, was called to the stand. After she was sworn in, the wife's attorney approached her and said, "For the record, will you please tell the court where the detective subpoenaed you."

The girl looked momentarily puzzled, but then brightened. "To the best of my recollection," she replied, "it was once in the canoe and twice in the hotel room!"

Here's a different kind of love story, about a farmer who let his crops wilt in the field in order to care for his deathly ill wife.

Day after day, he remained by her bedside. "I'm here for you, honey," he would say. "I love you."

One afternoon, however, the wife said in a weak voice, "I know you love me, but you've got to get the crops in."

He nodded. "You're right, honey, but I don't want to leave you."

"I'll be okay," the wife replied. "You can hire a nurse."

So the farmer hired a nurse, who came in every day and took care of his wife. She helped the wife in the bathroom, took her temperature, talked to her, and made sure she stayed warm and comfortable. After about a month, the wife showed signs of dramatic improvement, so the couple let the nurse go. Life returned to normal.

Three months later, the wife was preparing dinner while her husband went through the mail. She saw him open a letter and watched as his face went pale. "What is it?" she asked. "What's wrong?"

The farmer heaved a great sigh. "It's bad news, honey, but don't you worry about it."

"No," she replied, "I want to share the bad news."

"No," he said. "You don't want to know."

"Now see here," the wife said. "How long have we been married?"

"I guess about thirty-three years."

"That's right," the wife replied. "And do you remember what we did thirty-three years ago? We vowed that we would live life as one. So what hurts you hurts me. What saddens you saddens me. And if there's bad news it's *our* bad news. We took a vow, remember? Now I want you to tell me about that letter."

"Well," the farmer reluctantly began, "remember that nurse who was taking care of you when you were sick? Well, she writes here that it looks like *we* made her pregnant!"

Then there was the time this good old West Virginia boy was walking down a country road when he saw something glittering in the gravel. It was a mirror.

He lived so far out in the country, he'd never seen a mirror before! He looked at it and said, "How do you like that! It's a picture of my daddy! Now what would a person be doing leaving a picture of my daddy on a country road like that? How nice."

So he tucked the mirror inside his shirt and went back home with it.

The man decided that he didn't want to share his prize with his wife, so he crept into their bedroom, and slid the mirror underneath the mattress.

His wife, however, was spying on him as he hid the strange, glittering object. She waited until he went out to the barn to finish his chores, and then went into the bedroom and retrieved the mirror. She pulled it from beneath the mattress and stared into it.

"Oh!" she exclaimed angrily. "So that's the ugly old whore he's been running around with!"

Of course, not everyone living in West Virginia was quite so unsophisticated. I remember one family in particular, who had moved from the city to the country, that was rather well-to-do—a husband, a wife, and their little girl.

One day the little girl caught an eel in the backyard pond. While she was playing with the creature in her lap, the eel squirmed from her grasp. Quick as a wink, it swam up into her cooter and disappeared.

The little girl became hysterical. "Daddy! Mommy! Come quick!"

Her parents raced to their daughter and listened in astonishment as she told them what had occurred. Not entirely convinced, the parents nonetheless immediately called the family doctor. The doctor examined the girl and discovered, to his amazement, that there was indeed an eel coiled inside the girl. However, the doctor's repeated attempts to remove it failed.

"There's only one thing to do," he told the distraught parents. "We have to get one of those well-endowed country boys to come over here and knock the bottom out of your daughter!"

The parents gasped at the thought of their little daughter being hobbled, but the doctor was adamant. "It's the only way to get the job done." When that eel sees those hydraulics, it will think it's a female eel and wrap itself around it, trying to mate!"

The parents were in anguish over the doctor's prescription. The mother collapsed in a chair, crying, and the father paced up and down the living room.

The father suddenly stopped his pacing. "I've got it!" he shouted. "You know that strapping half-wit who lives down the road? I bet he's pretty well endowed. And if he told anybody about this, nobody would believe him because he's a half-wit."

So the father and the doctor got hold of the half-wit and brought him to the house. They led him upstairs and closed the door to their daughter's bedroom. He started pouring the coal to that cooler.

Five minutes after entering the daughter's bedroom, the half-wit came barreling out of the room with that black eel wrapped completely around his hydraulics! Screaming at the top of his lungs, the fellow ran out the front door, down the road, and disappeared into the distance.

Several years later, the local boys were sitting in a bar shooting the breeze when the girl's name came up. "Yeah," one of the country boys said, "she's high society. I wonder what it would be like to cut a slice of that."

The half-wit was sitting in a corner, drinking a beer. "I know what it's like," he said, a crazy grin on his face.

The other guys looked at him in stunned silence, then they all bust out laughing.

"Well, what was it like?" asked one of the boys, humoring him. "Was it tight?"

"Yeah, it was tight," the half-wit replied. "It was so tight it pinched the hydraulics off the guy before me!"

Same as in all rural areas, West Virginians really love their farm animals. One afternoon, I was out for a drive when I came across a bunch of people running along the shoulder of the road. They were all smiling and laughing.

I rolled down my window. "Hey," I shouted at one old farmer. "What's all the action about?"

"Ain't you heard?" he yelled back. "It's the annual sheep shearing festival!"

I'd never been to a sheep shearing festival, so I decided to see what it was all about. I parked the car and followed the crowd to a big barn. A banner outside proclaimed, "Sheep Shearing Festival Today!"

I stood in line to get a ticket. Off to my right, I saw a guy wailing away right out there, in front of God and everybody.

"What the hell are you doing?" I yelled at him.

"It's the sheep shearing festival!" he yelled back. "I'm so excited I just can't control myself!"

Unbelievable! I finally got my ticket and went inside, where an excited crowd square-danced and drank corn liquor. Everyone was laughing and whooping it up, celebrating like it was the Fourth of July and New Year's Eve rolled into one.

I spotted a couple of good old boys having a frantic wailing contest beside the bleachers. This was just too much. I walked over to a fellow standing off to the side, sipping on his own private jug of moonshine. "What in the world is going on here?" I asked him.

"You're a city boy, ain't you?" he said. "So you've probably never been to a sheep shearing festival before."

"You're right," I said. "What's the big deal?"

"What's the big deal?" he cried. "It means we get to see them *naked!*"

I was so unnerved by the festival activities that I ran to my car and started to drive home. Flustered, I ran smack dab into a goat and killed him. I stopped on the side of the road and just sat there, trying to pull myself together.

And They Ask Me Why I Drink?

Suddenly, a farmer came running over. "Dammit," he yelled. "I saw you, city boy. You killed my goat."

I got out of the car and tried to calm him. "Easy, sir, easy! Don't worry! I'll replace your goat!"

"All right," he said, with a sigh of relief. "In that case, pull your pants down and lie over that fence!"

CALLER: *I heard a rumor somewhere that you were an opera singer in one of your previous career explorations.*

GREASEMAN: *It's true. I did a lot of stuff before becoming host of this show. However, during my one and only appearance at Carnegie Hall, I never got to sing. I was drummed off the stage—booed and hissed at. The maestro and the musicians called it a disrespectful performance. So I offer a word of warning to anyone contemplating an operatic singing career:* If you want to get into opera, never eat at Benny's Burrito Barn prior to a performance!

Chapter 9

My Brilliant Part-Time Careers

I returned to New York from West Virginia with an entirely fresh appreciation of life—city life, that is. I moved back in with my parents in the Bronx and set out to get a job.

If there's one thing my parents instilled in me as a child, it was that there's no such thing as a free lunch. I've always worked. As a little boy, I mowed grass and ran errands. When I was in high school, I always had a part-time job, and I worked my way through college, too. As a result of these experiences, most of them brief, I've gained an incredible amount of knowledge about a variety of people, places, and things.

Although my goal was to be on the radio, I briefly had a job as an office manager in a small insurance agency. I'll never forget it because my first task was to hire a secretary.

Oh my God.

This applicant came in for an interview and ohhh-h-h, was she schweet! I looked at her and my jaw dropped. No kidding: All you could hear was the flippity-flop of saliva as it cascaded over my lower lip.

"I'm here to apply for the secretarial position," she said. She removed her coat and displayed a perfectly matched pair of rounded, size C ta-tas.

"Fine!" I said. "We'll begin with a test of your secretarial skills.

"So," I smiled, "let's start with dictation. I want you to take down everything I say—your shirt, your nylons, your panties, your . . ."

Despite the insurance company's strict rule against interoffice action, she was one secretary I couldn't resist. I was putting the stones to her on a regular basis, so we had to be very careful. We worked out a code so that we wouldn't get caught. When I wanted her to come to my office so we could do a little bottom knocking, I'd get on the office intercom and say, "Miss Nelson, I need you in my office, please. I have to write a letter to Mr. Sexton."

One day I summoned her over the intercom, but she got on the loudspeaker system and replied, "I'm sorry, Mr. Mannelli, I can't write a letter to Mr. Sexton today. I have the red ribbon in my typewriter."

A day later she was feeling frisky again. "Mr. Mannelli,"

she announced over the loudspeaker, "I'm ready to write a letter to Mr. Sexton today."

I picked up the phone. "I'm sorry, Miss Nelson," I explained. "But I've already written him by *hand!*"

My career in insurance was put on permanent hold after my boss cracked the code. I looked for another job, and wound up an administrative assistant to the owner of a manufacturing company.

One time the boss was interviewing a new salesperson, who was definitely triple schweet. As she walked into his office, the boss gave me a wink and closed the door. A couple of minutes later, I heard the sounds of sweaty romping.

Just then the phone rang. It was the boss's wife.

"Is my husband in?" she sweetly inquired.

"Just a second," I replied. "Let me check."

With the phone still in hand, I went over to the keyhole and peeked into the room. "Yes," I reported, "he's in! No, he's out. He's in, he's out, he's in . . . !!"

I guess the wife was *not* amused. The next day I was fired. I wasn't bothered; secretarial jobs were a dime a dozen. I knew I was destined to do something new and different, something that would tap into my (admittedly incredible) potential.

It didn't take me long to figure out that my next job wasn't my destiny, either. I became a long-distance trucker, and spent a year driving from Chicago to Omaha to Denver and then back again.

It was a pretty boring trip, so I looked forward to having the company inspector accompany me every few months. He was there to make sure you drove safely, and that your big rig was up-to-date.

And They Ask Me Why I Drink?

One night I was driving along, with the inspector sitting alongside me with his clipboard. He was taking notes, making remarks about my driving, when I realized we were nearing the next truck stop.

"Tell you what," I said. "This is the hottest truck stop in the country. They've got hookers working the parking lot, and the second you pull your rig in, they come up and ask if you want a little action! What do you say we stop? We can get a couple of good snarlings *and* a good meal!"

The inspector put down his pen and stared at me. "Good God, man," he sneered. "I'll have you know I've got more than I can handle at home!"

"Oh," I said. "Then let's go over to your place!"

Another job had me working in the advertising department of the local newspaper, in charge of the romantic classifieds.

One afternoon this little old spinster woman walked in. "I'd like to take out an ad," she said. "I want to meet somebody."

"No problem, ma'am!" I said. "It's five dollars per insertion."

"Really?" she said, her eyes widening. "Well, here's twenty dollars, *and to hell with the ad!*"

My next job was at a drugstore. Friday nights were definitely the weirdest. One guy would stroll in every Friday night and buy two dozen condoms. No pack of smokes. No magazine. Nothing.

Only condoms.

This continued for two months. Finally, I couldn't take the suspense any longer. The next Friday night I said, "Buddy, you must be really tearing it up! Two dozen condoms a week? You're my hero!"

"How dare you assume that," he answered with surprising irritation, "that I, as you so crudely put it, am 'tearing it up.' My purchase has nothing whatsoever to do with sex. I have trained my French poodle to swallow these condoms. Now when he takes a massive, it comes out in a nice little plastic bag!"

One summer I drove a bus for Bellevue Hospital. That was before these days of political correctness. Back then, Bellevue was known simply as "the nuthouse."

My job was to transport dysfunctional guys. While they weren't a danger to the public, they weren't quite ready to rejoin society. I took them on various outings and affectionately referred to them as "our nuts."

Once I drove a group of them to Yankee Stadium to attend a baseball game. My guys took up two whole rows.

Just as the game was getting ready to start, I had to go to the men's room.

I didn't know what to do. I was afraid to leave my nuts unsupervised, but I was really desperate to make my bladder gladder. I glanced around to see if there was someone who could help me out.

This guy came lumbering along, and I grabbed him. "Hey, buddy, could you help me out?" I asked urgently, and explained the situation.

"What do you want me to do?" he said. "I'm not used to dealing with those people."

"Look, they'd be fine by themselves," I said.

"The only thing I'm worried about is when the National Anthem starts. They won't know when to stand up or when to sit down. So could you just yell 'Up nuts!' and then 'Down nuts' at the appropriate times? They're really pretty mellow, so you shouldn't have a problem."

"It sounds easy enough," he said. "Okay, I'll do it."

"Great! I'll be right back."

I wasn't gone ten minutes, but by the time I returned the stadium was in a state of pandemonium. People were throwing things at each other! Fistfights had broken out!

I grabbed the guy I'd left in charge.

"My God," I yelled. "What happened?"

He shook his head. "I don't know exactly how to explain it. Everything was perfectly fine. The National Anthem started. I yelled 'Up nuts' and they all stood up. When the Anthem ended, I yelled 'Down nuts!' And they all sat down. Then this vendor came walking through the crowd, yelling 'Peanuts!', and that was that!"

My next job found me working as head usher at Radio City Music Hall in New York City.

It was just a couple of weeks before Christmas, and the Music Hall was jammed with people eager to see The Rockettes and the big holiday show. Adding to the chaos, half of our ushers came down with the flu, leaving us shorthanded.

Management collectively flipped out. "What are we going to do? We need somebody at all the entrances and exits! Help!"

I had no choice but to take matters into my own hands.

I glanced down the street and saw a guy holding a sign: "Will Work for Food." I decided to take him up on the offer.

"Hey, you!" I yelled. "How would you like to make a day's pay?"

He dropped the sign and ran over.

"We're short ushers. Here—put this uniform on and clean yourself up. You can use the men's room downstairs."

"Okay," the guy said, "but I don't know anything about ushering."

"It's easy! All you've got to do is stand by the theater entrance. When people come in, just tell them to move to the right. Got that? Tell them to move to the right!"

About fifteen minutes later, people started flooding into the Music Hall, and my recruit started off just fine. "Move to the right," he announced in a clear voice. "Ladies and gentlemen, move to the right."

I was real pleased. Everything was going smoothly— until this old lady in elegant attire walked in.

"Please move to the right," my homeless usher said.

"There must be some mistake," the woman said with some annoyance. "I have a mezzanine box."

"Lady," the guy replied, "I don't care if you have chrome-plated ta-tas. Move to the right!"

Before I landed the Radio City Music Hall job, I had a similar gig at a less prestigious theater—a triple XXX theater in Times Square. I was standing at the entrance to the joint one night, checking the batteries in my flashlight and plying God knows what from the bottom of my shoes, when this elderly couple entered.

Startled by their appearance, I watched them escort each other down the aisle to their seats. They sat right in the middle of the theater.

After the movie ended, I expected to see them leave, but they didn't. After fifteen minutes, I decided to walk down to where they were sitting to see what was going on.

"Excuse me, folks," I said. "I couldn't help but see you come in—and I couldn't help but wonder what you thought of the movie."

The husband looked up at me, disgust written all over

his face. "It was horrible," he said. "It was the most repugnant thing I ever saw in my life."

His wife nodded in agreement. "It was sick."

"I don't mean any disrespect," I said, "but you *did* sit through the entire movie. Why didn't you leave?"

"We couldn't," the wife explained. "We had to wait until the lights came up. *My* panties were off and *his* teeth were out!"

Since I had so much experience working with people, I thought I'd try my hand as a counselor. One of my clients was a homosexual. We often talked about how being gay affected him. We were walking through the park one morning, having a fine talk, when he suddenly stopped.

"Whoops," he said. "I feel the rumblings of a massive coming on." He ducked behind a bush.

And then he started screaming. I darted back there to see what had happened. His pants were still down, and he was staring at the massive on the ground.

"What's wrong?" I asked.

"I had a miscarriage."

"You can't have had a miscarriage—you can't have a baby!"

"Look! There's tiny arms and tiny legs in my massive!"

"You idiot," I said. "You just crapped on a frog!"

So much for social work.

After that, I signed a three-month contract to work as a roughneck on an oil rig in Mexico. The job paid big bucks, but you worked every day, seven days a week. When those three months were over, I needed a woman *bad!*

I flew into Tijuana on my way back to the States. I grabbed a taxi and, in my broken Spanish, conveyed to the driver that I was looking for a little action. He responded that the best place was Madam Luchicas, and he drove me there in short order.

I walked through the door and went right up to the Madam herself.

"I've been working hard for three months," I said. "I want you to send the biggest, toughest hooker you've got in this place up to my room. I've got a lot of pent-up action, so she'd better be tough enough to handle it."

I started off to my room and paused to add one more thing. "And have her bring up a couple of bottles of beer too!"

I went to the room, took a long, hot shower, and lay on the bed naked, with my hands folded behind my head. Suddenly, the door swung open with such force that the hinges broke! Standing in the portal was a huge, nude woman. She must have been at least six and a half feet tall, and at least two hundred pounds. She was covered with horrible scars and tattoos.

Equally important, she was carrying two bottles of beer.

Without saying a word, she walked up to me, handed me the bottles, and then dropped down on all fours on the floor.

"Wait a minute," I said. "Get up here on the bed. I'm not into that kinky stuff!"

"Oh," she said. "I'm sorry, *señor!* I thought maybe you wanted to open up the beer bottles *first!*"

The next morning I crossed the border into California, thumbed my way to Wyoming, and got a job as a mechanic.

One dark night a woman drove up, got out of her car, and came into the office. "Are you the mechanic?" she asked.

I nodded.

"My husband asked me to bring the car by while he's at work," she said. "He wants it checked out from top to bottom."

"Okay. Let me see what shape it's in."

I popped the hood and started fiddling with the engine. I was wearing a sweaty T-shirt that stuck to my body, and I guess she noted my well-developed arms working the wrenches, my powerful shoulders heaving to and fro. The next thing I knew, she had moved closer and her body was brushing up against mine.

I turned to her with a grease-covered hand, lifted her chin and kissed her full on the lips. She returned my passion, literally tearing the T-shirt from my body. I grabbed her around the waist, carried her to the backseat of the car, and we began tearing it up. She was a wildcat!

We were in the midst of this zesty session when the cellular phone in the front seat of the car began to ring. I tried to ignore it but the incessant ringing finally got to me. I grabbed the receiver.

"Hello!" I yelled.

"How's my car coming along?" the woman's husband asked.

"Just fine, sir," I replied. "In fact, we're testing the shocks right now!"

I got a crick in my neck that day that just wouldn't go away, so I dialed up a massage parlor and made an appointment. I hurried over, and the receptionist led me to a small room. I got naked and flopped onto the table.

I was laying there, feeling the tingle of the doodads, when the masseuse entered. "All right," she said, "keep in mind we have an honest business here. All we offer is a standard rubdown. So before we get started, is there anything I can help you with?"

"Yeah!" I said, jumping off the table. "You can help me get my damn clothes back on!"

Part II

Here Comes the Bride (That Pig, Estelle)

CALLER: *My ex-wife, she's been deviling me for fifteen years. Now my son, who is fourteen, is telling me he don't want to see me anymore. What should I do?*
GREASEMAN: *Start drinking.*

Chapter 10

Estelle: My Big Mistake

For a long time I didn't think I was ever going to get married. The first girl I really fell for was named Cindy. After we'd dated for several months, I brought her home to introduce her to Momma and Daddy.

"Cindy and I are engaged," I announced. Momma looked happy but Daddy looked upset. He asked me to step outside with him for a minute.

We went into the backyard. "I've got to be honest with you, son. You can't marry Cindy."

I was dumbstruck. "Why not?"

"Well, you see," Daddy explained, "when I was young, I used to fool around a lot and, uh, I was with Cindy's mom. She's your half sister, son."

Crestfallen, I dumped Cindy without telling her why.

I didn't date for months after that. Then I met Veronica and fell in love again. She was beautiful. She had flaxen hair, mischievous eyes, and a body straight from heaven. We dated for a year, then got engaged.

And They Ask Me Why I Drink?

She came home with me to announce our engagement to my parents. Just as I was getting ready to tell them the news, Daddy took me aside.

"Son," he said softly, "I hate to tell you this, but you can't marry Veronica. I know this is hard to believe, but Veronica's your half sister, too!"

Like Cindy, I dumped Veronica without explanation. Again I stopped dating. Watching me sulk around the house day after day was too much for Momma. Finally, she put her arm around my shoulders.

"Nino," she said. "Why are you looking so sad?"

"Momma," I confided, "I don't think I'm ever going to get married. I fell in love with Cindy, but then Daddy told me she was my illegitimate half sister. I fell in love with Veronica, and Daddy said that she was my half sister too!"

Momma smiled. "You'll get married someday, Nino, I promise. Don't let your father bother you. To be perfectly honest with you, son, I fooled around too, and, well, he's not your natural father!"

I eventually met and married Estelle. Okay, she wasn't pretty, but she had money. But it's just like they say—when you marry for money, one way or another, you end up paying.

And Lord, how I paid!

Estelle Ochingurtis, half-Scottish, half-German. She was a lumbering 5'10" tall, if she was an inch. I'll never forget the night Estelle and I got engaged. It was Christmas Eve. Instead of buying her a gift *and* a ring, I decided to kill two presents with one bill and just get her the ring.

We were enjoying an intimate dinner at her place that night, and I thought I'd get cute. While Estelle was in the

kitchen putting the finishing touches on our chateaubri-
and, I put her engagement ring in a glass of champagne.

She came out of the kitchen and sat down at the table.
We began to eat. I waited for Estelle to notice the ring in
the glass, but she didn't. I realized that the lights—
dimmed to enhance the romantic mood—were so low
that Estelle couldn't see the ring.

I suggested a Christmas toast. I figured that when she
went to lift her glass, she'd see it for sure.

We lifted our glasses. "Happiness to both of us, and to
everyone throughout the land," I said, and we clinked our
glasses. Suddenly, without a pause, Estelle threw back her
glass of champagne—and swallowed the ring.

She began to choke and her eyes started bugging out of
her head. Realizing that her windpipe was blocked by the
ring, I jumped up from the table, and quickly performed
the Heimlich Maneuver. I picked her up, swung her
around, and her feet hit the Christmas tree. The tree
toppled over and all the water in the stand spilled out on
the floor. The Christmas tree lights started to buzz and
short-circuit. Throughout all of this, I was thumping her
on the back.

Finally, out of sheer desperation, I hit her as hard as I
could. She swallowed the ring.

I opened her yap, and stuck my hand in there. "Where is
it?" I yelled. "That ring cost me thirty-seven hundred
dollars! Don't move, Estelle! Don't move!"

I had to give up. I left Estelle panting on the floor and
called the emergency room of the nearby medical center.

"I just proposed to my girlfriend," I said, "and I put the
engagement ring in a glass of champagne and she swallowed it! Is there anything you can do? Should I bring her
over?"

And They Ask Me Why I Drink?

The nurse snorted. "Frankly, young man, I don't think there's a doctor in the country who would operate just to get a wedding ring out of your girlfriend's intestinal track. She's just going to have to pass it herself. You're just going to have to wait for nature to run its course!"

"Pass it? As in a massive?"

"Exactly!"

Discouraged, disgusted, and depressed, I hung up the phone. "Thirty-seven hundred bucks," I muttered under my breath. I looked at Estelle. "Everything's going to be okay," I told her. "This, too, shall pass!"

Right before our wedding, I sat Estelle down on the couch and gently patted her hand. "Estelle," I said. "I think it's time that you and I revealed all our past sex partners."

"But Nino," she said, "we did that two weeks ago!"

"Yeah," I said, "but that was *two weeks* ago!"

My decision to marry Estelle was a snap judgment. I was getting ready to ship out to Vietnam and getting hitched to Estelle before I left seemed like the thing to do. I rushed into marriage without even thinking about the ramifications of spending the rest of my life with this woman. And God, what a mistake!

Of course, I didn't realize it was a mistake immediately.

The first tip-off came when I returned from Nam. I stood in the doorway in all my battle regalia, my ribbons shining on my chest. My skin was still smarting from the shrapnel, and the spit from antiwar protesters was still stuck on the side of my face.

I walked in, threw my duffel bag down in the hallway, and said, "Estelle, what's this I hear about Arnie Schmultz nailing every woman in this neighborhood except for one?"

"Oh," Estelle sneered, "it's got to be that holier-than-thou Mrs. Markowitz!"

Over the years, many people have asked me, "Grease, why in the world did you marry Estelle?" The answer is very simple. I married her for the money. A man has to go where the cash is, and Estelle came from a very wealthy family. I stupidly decided to marry her because she had some cash, and she *never* let me forget it.

We'd be driving along in our big old Eldorado, and she'd smile as she settled back into the plush leather seats. "You know," she'd say, "I love this car. If it weren't for my money, we'd never have it."

We'd pull up in front of our huge, luxurious house with the tennis court and swimming pool and she'd say, "Man, oh, man, what a beautiful house. Of course, if it weren't for my money, we'd never have been able to afford it."

I'd go inside, grab a beer, and try to ignore her by sitting in front of the big screen TV that took up half the room. But ignoring Estelle was an impossible task.

I turned on the television one lazy Saturday afternoon, and was getting ready to watch the ball game when she came into the living room. "Just look at those football players!" she exclaimed. "They look like they're right here in the room with us. That sure is a hell of a TV set. Of course, if it weren't for my money, it wouldn't be here."

At that point I jumped up from the couch. "Estelle, let me be honest with you. *If it weren't for your money, I wouldn't be here!*"

I should have known that Estelle was no good, that she was cheating on me, but I was stupid. I was blind! It wasn't until we moved from Jacksonville to Washington that I became really suspicious. After all, we still had the same milkman!

I suppose I should have known that her affairs bode of some sort of medical condition, because the sickest thing she did to make me feel inadequate was to make certain I knew about her dalliances.

Estelle was always in need of some new kind of thrill. She grabbed a bag of birdseed one day, sprinkled it all over her body, and then had our parakeet peck her into ecstasy!

Since the bearded clam is not designed for this type of activity, the following day Estelle was agonizingly sore and raw. She went to the doctor and explained what she'd done with the birdseed and the parakeet. "Look at this," she said, lifting her dress and dropping her panties. "Just look at *this!*"

The doctor took a look. "My God, you have twerpes!"

"Is it bad?" Estelle cried.

"Bad?" the doctor replied. "Why, it's *untweetable!*"

Despite her infidelities, Estelle and I still made love. One night we made love for at least thirty-five minutes. The slap, slap, slap of the doodads filled the night air.

I was soaked with sweat when I finally achieved Shangri-la. I rolled over onto my side of the bed. Estelle sat up and looked at me.

"That's amazing, Nino," she said. "We've been married for five years and you still make love to me for thirty-five minutes! You must *really* love me!"

I looked at her through the rivulets of sweat dripping from my forehead. "Naw," I said. "I just couldn't think of anybody else!"

* * *

Although I think we both knew the marriage was doomed, we tried to salvage it. We undertook behavior modification. We joined est. We tried the hot tubs at Essalen. Nothing seemed to help. Then I read about Tom Arnold, and how he'd had Roseanne's face tattooed on his chest. I thought maybe, just maybe, this could be the answer to our problems.

I went to a tattoo parlor and had "I LOVE YOU" tattooed on my hydraulics in a rainbow of colors. Do you realize the agony and humiliation I had to endure?

It was one of those tattoo parlors where you sit in the window to attract other customers. It was totally demeaning. People would walk by and stare. "Hey, look at this guy," they'd yell. "Look at the size of those avocado doodads!"

What a fool I was. I waited until the tattoo had healed up real nicely, then surprised Estelle with it one night. She was in the bathroom and I was lying in bed. When she walked into the room I threw back the covers and yelled, "Surprise, Estelle! Look at this!"

She walked over to the bed and read the tattoo. "There you go again, Nino. Always trying to put words in my mouth!"

One afternoon I came home early from work to find a Maserati, a Porsche, a Mercedes, and a Cadillac in the driveway.

Thinking Estelle was having a Tupperware party or a ladies' bridge game, I tiptoed through the front door. Imagine my surprise when I saw Estelle splayed on the couch, surrounded by a group of doctors wearing nothing but white lab coats and stethoscopes. There must have been twelve of them, all with their pants down. They were encircling her on the couch.

And They Ask Me Why I Drink?

I stood in the doorway and watched this scene in total disbelief. "My God, Estelle!" I screamed. "When you told me you wanted to dedicate your body to science, I thought you meant *after you were dead!*"

I suppose there were a lot of factors contributing to our breakup. There was Estelle's nymphomania, and I guess, to be perfectly honest, there was my selfishness. I wasn't *always* selfish, mind you. In the beginning of our relationship, I tried to give Estelle everything she desired. One time we were shopping at the neighborhood mall. Estelle saw this eleven-hundred-dollar couch and decided she couldn't live without it.

I balked at the purchase. "It's too expensive."

"If you buy this couch for me," Estelle said. "You won't have to buy me a Christmas present."

I bought the couch and immediately regretted it. It was a pain in the *tokhis* from the moment it was delivered.

I'd come home from work, exhausted, flop down on the couch, and light up a Camel. As if by magic, Estelle would suddenly appear in the doorway.

"My God," she'd cry, "don't smoke on my brand-new couch. You'll burn a hole in it!"

On the weekends, I'd be watching a ball game and decide to take a little nap. No sooner would I sling my legs up on the couch to stretch out than Estelle would fly into the room. "Get your feet off that couch!" she'd yell.

On other occasions Estelle wouldn't say a word. Instead, she'd spot me on the couch and just walk up and slap me upside the head.

She nearly drove me crazy with that couch. "Change your clothes," she'd command. "Put on your bathrobe before you sit on that couch."

One day I felt the flu coming on, so I left work early. I

walked through the front door to find the lovely Estelle, self-proclaimed defender of the living room couch, sitting naked on the object of her concern. Her legs were splayed wide open, allowing some guy I'd never seen to feast on the yeast.

I marched over to that couch and grabbed that guy by his hair.

"Wait just a minute!" I said. "My wife won't let me put my feet on that couch and here you are *eating off of it!*"

Speaking of eating, Estelle's pathetic cooking didn't help our situation. I remember opening day of quail season years ago. I was still married to Estelle and she was giving me hell about going hunting with the guys. As I walked out the front door, she hurled her final insult: "How can you shoot those pretty little things?"

"Look," I told her, "they're God's bounty. I'm going out to harvest game and you're going to cook it when I get back."

My buddies and I did some good shooting and got our bag limits. We decided to go back to my house and have a big quail dinner. When we arrived home, I went out in the backyard, plucked the quail, and told Estelle to cook them up.

An hour or so later we all sat down to dinner. The quail were hideous-tasting—hideous! Regardless, everyone made a valiant effort to eat them. Finally, I slammed down my fork.

"Guys," I said, "you don't have to eat these. They're terrible!"

I turned to Estelle. "What in the blue blazes did you stuff these birds with?"

"Nothing," she said. "They weren't hollow!"

* * *

And They Ask Me Why I Drink?

I think Daddy and his perverse behavior also contributed to our marital woes. Not long after I married Estelle, Momma finally got fed up with Daddy's antics, and kicked him out. Daddy moved into a double-wide trailer with his sometime girlfriend, Trixie Hicks. I was curious about Trixie, and also about how Daddy was getting along, so I went over for a visit.

"You take a look around," Daddy said as soon as the screen door banged behind me, "and you tell me this ain't living!"

He had a big old settee strategically placed directly in front of the TV set in the living room, and all kinds of chips and dips on the coffee table. "If you think this is something," he said, "wait 'til you see my art room!"

"Art room?"

"Yessirree!" He laughed. "My art room!"

He took me to the back of the double-wide and into an addition that was filled with nothing but statues of women in various poses. As I stood there, dumbfounded, Daddy went over to a statue of a headless, legless female torso.

He strapped it on and started hobbling away. "Daddy," I cried, "what are you doing?"

He looked over his shoulder at me and smiled. "Well, son, you know I've always said art should be functional!"

Daddy was fired from his job on the loading dock. Weeks turned into months and he still wasn't able to find work.

When he finally ran out of money and couldn't afford to live with Trixie anymore, he came over to see me. "Son," he said, "I've got to stay in your extra bedroom. I know it's not the best of living arrangements, but you wouldn't turn me out, would you?"

When Estelle and I would go to bed at night, Daddy

would be in the living room, the television set blaring. I'd come downstairs in the morning and find him passed out on the couch, half a pizza pie lying on his belly, a pile of beer cans on the coffee table.

This wasn't a pretty sight to begin with, but it only got worse when he'd invite his women friends over.

One weekend Estelle and I had invited her parents over for dinner, and had picked them up on our way back from the shopping mall. The four of us came bounding through the front door and Daddy was there—with some hussy. He was on the living room couch, burying face in front of God and everybody!

I was so shocked I didn't know what to do. Daddy, of course, was totally unperturbed by our presence. He just waved and continued with what he was doing.

Estelle's mother, on the other hand, nearly fainted. Her father was visibly shaken and Estelle was furious.

"That's it, Nino! He has to go!"

Estelle guided her parents out of the room in a huff. I threw a blanket over the woman, grabbed Daddy by the hair, and dragged him out into the backyard. "Daddy," I said, "we've got to talk. You have got to get some counseling. There's nothing wrong with having a date, but you've got to know when and where to have them. You've got to show some control!"

I gave Daddy an ultimatum. "I'm making an appointment for you with a psychiatrist. If you don't go, then you're going to have to live elsewhere!"

I guess my threat scared him because Daddy kept the appointment. When he returned home, however, he was all smiles.

"What did the psychiatrist say?" I asked.

"He said there's nothing much wrong with me," Daddy

replied with a big grin. "I've just got me an *eat-a-puss complex*, that's all!"

Estelle and I decided to take a trip to Mexico to get away from my crazy Daddy, and everybody else as well. Our marriage was in trouble. I was looking forward to lying on the beach and drinking Margaritas, but Estelle was unhappy with that plan.

"Some of the greatest wonders of the world are here in Mexico," she said. "I want to see the waterfall of Diddegoopa."

"I don't want to see any damn waterfall," I moaned.

"But Nino, all we ever do is waddle from the hotel to the beach and back to the hotel! Come on, let's go sight-seeing!"

I couldn't stand Estelle's constant complaining, so I gave in. We rented a rattletrap car, and started driving. Soon we were in the middle of mountainous nowhere. Eventually the car couldn't go any further, and just conked out.

None of this phased Estelle. "I know we're close to the waterfall," she said. "Let's just walk there."

We left the car in the middle of the dirt road and started out on foot. We'd gone about a mile when, suddenly, in the distance up ahead, I saw a man leading a horse down the trail.

"Hey, *señor*," I yelled. "*Donde por favor . . .*"

"*Señor*," he replied. "I speak English. How can I help you?"

"We're lost. We're looking for the waterfall of Diddegoopa."

"*Señor*, I've just come from there! I was getting some corn feed for my horse. It's about a half-mile walk. If you follow the piles of horse manure with the corn in it, the trail will take you right to the waterfall."

"Thanks a lot," I said. "Hear that, Estelle? We just have to follow the horse manure with the corn."

So Estelle and I began following the clumps of manure. I was bent over, practically on my hands and knees, because there was a lot of manure on the trail, but not all of it was studded with corn. When we had walked about halfway there, another guy came along. He stopped alongside me.

"*Gringo*," he said, "can I help you?"

"Yes," I said. "I'm looking for horse manure with corn in it."

"With corn in it?" he exclaimed. "Gringo, if you're *that* hungry, here—take a bit of my taco!"

We were staying at a small hotel in the town of Impreagua, somewhere outside Acapulco. After the disaster at the waterfall, followed by a full course of Estelle's nagging, I decided I had to get away from the woman, at least for a few hours, and the ocean seemed my only avenue of escape. I called down to the front desk and told the manager I'd like to do a little spear fishing.

"Okay, *Señor Gringo*," the manager said. "I will send a man up immediately."

I turned to Estelle. "Amuse yourself this afternoon. I'm going spear fishing."

There was a knock on the door. It was the guide. He took a long look at me. "Okay," he said. "First we must tweeze the eyebrows."

Tweeze the eyebrows? I thought. What the hell is this? I figured it had something to do with the swim mask I'd be wearing.

But then he said, *"Sí,* and put a little rouge on your cheeks."

Rouge on my cheeks? Well, I thought, maybe it scares away some dangerous underwater fish.

"Okay," the guide said after applying the rouge. "Now I must put the lipstick on you."

At this point, I was really puzzled, but I complied. I pursed my lips, and let the guy put the lipstick on me. After he was finished, he stood back and took a long, approving look.

"Now," he said, "I put these earrings in your left ear, and in your right ear. Oh, that is very nice. I think also we will give you an extra-close shave so your skin is smooth and silky."

After shaving me, the guide stood back and gave me another approving nod. "Now, *señor,* if you would please step out of that seersucker and put on these crotchless panties."

"Crotchless panties?" I yelled. "All this for *spear fishing?"*

The guide looked at me quizzically. *"Spear fishing?* I thought you said *'queer fishing!' "*

It was during this same vacation that I had a terrible bout of dysentery, a gut-rumbling case of Montezuma's worst revenge. I couldn't get myself off the porcelain convenience for more than ten minutes at a time. I guess I'd overdone it my first day there by consuming forty burritos, four cheese enchiladas, countless chile rellenos—and buckets of warm, Mexican tap water. By early evening, my belly had begun percolating some serious butt coffee.

I wasn't any better the next day, so I went to the doctor.

"This is the worst case of dysentery I've ever seen," he said.

"This is beyond the help of normal medicine. You better go see the witch doctor."

I took a cab to the witch doctor's *casa*, with my *tokhis* hanging out the back window. This time I left a trail of my own. When we finally got there, I ran to the witch doctor's front door. "You've gotta help me, *Señor* Witch Doctor!" I cried.

"I will help you, *gringo*," he said, "but first you must come out to my field."

"The first thing I want you to do," he said once we were out there, "is walk fifty yards east. Then I want you to take two steps north and then walk fifty yards west. Take your pants off and do what comes naturally while you are walking."

Figuring this was some kind of magical cure—a sort of "salutation" to the god of dysentery—I obliged.

I dropped my pants and I started walking fifty yards here, fifty yards there, leaving a hideous, messy trail behind me.

After about an hour of this, I yelled to the witch doctor, who was sitting in the shade of a nearby tree, "Hey, is this really working?"

"It's working for me, *gringo*," he yelled back. "You are *fertilizing my garden very nicely!*"

After that last experience south of the border, Estelle and I flew to Australia for ten days of first-class sight-seeing and holiday fun.

After touring Sydney, we rented a Range Rover and headed for the Australian Outback.

I was driving down this godforsaken dirt road when a kangaroo jumped out of the scrubs in front of us. We were absolutely enthralled. I stopped the car and Estelle started rolling her video camera.

As she was filming, a guy ran out from behind the bushes. He grabbed the kangaroo and began pouring the coal to it.

Estelle nearly fainted. "Don't just stay here," she said, "drive!"

As I pulled away, I looked in the rear view. The guy was really tearing that kangaroo a new one.

"I feel nauseous," Estelle said. "What a horrible, perverted man!"

We drove along and soon saw someone on horseback way up ahead. As we came closer, I realized the guy was chasing a kangaroo, trying to lasso it. I slowed the car down, and we watched, mesmerized, as the guy roped and hogtied it like a calf. He flipped it around and started hobbling the animal, right in front of us.

Estelle vomited out the window.

"Look," I said, "there's a small town just a few miles up ahead. What do you say we stop and get a cold beer or something?"

We headed into town and stopped at the first bar we encountered.

"Gooday!" I said to the bartender. "How ya doing, buddy! Would you draw us a couple of cold beers?" I turned to Estelle. "I'm going to the bathroom to splash a little cold water on my face."

I walked to the back of the bar and went into the men's room. A guy with a peg leg was standing in front of the urinal, just wailing away and smiling.

I ran back out to the bar. "Hey," I said to the bartender. "What's with the deviant in the bathroom? What the hell kind of place are you people running here anyway?"

The bartender looked at me and smiled. "Show some

consideration," he said. "You don't expect a man with a peg leg to run down a kangaroo, do you?"

Toward the end of our marriage, Estelle would go her way and I would go mine, especially on weekends. We'd only see each other in passing during the week. We reached a point where we didn't care what the other was doing.

One night shortly before the marriage ended, I was half-liquored up and heading home. It was about three o'clock in the morning. As I drove I tried to think up an excuse to give Estelle for being so late. Suddenly, like a gift from God, an entire story began forming in my sodden brain:

I decided to tell her I'd received an emergency call from work. Someone at the plant had suffered a heart attack, and I had had to accompany him to the hospital. Then I had to locate the next of kin to get permission for the heart transplant that would save his life.

I felt so good about the tale that, instead of tiptoeing into the bedroom as I usually did, I just opened the door and walked in. Imagine my surprise when I discovered Estelle in bed with another man.

I stood there in the doorway, boiling mad. "How do you like that," I muttered angrily to myself. "Wouldn't you know it would be on the night I have a *good* excuse for being late!"

Looking back, I realize Estelle and I were doomed from day one. We always had rotten luck. We got married too young and were too different from the start. With time, we only grew further and further apart, until, finally, we had nothing in common and no respect for one another.

I began calling her "Canyon Cooter," and she began referring to me as "Skeeter Tweeter."

"You know our marriage is shot," she said.

"Yeah, I know."

She sat there quietly for a moment. "Tell you what I'll do. I'll play you one hand of gin rummy. If you win, we get divorced. If I win, you've got to come to marital counseling with me. Will you play?"

"By all means," I replied, "but why don't we make it a penny a point, just to make it interesting!"

CALLER: *Grease, I'm hating life. My wife and I are at each other's throats.*

GREASEMAN: *That reminds me of what Daddy used to say: Marriage is like getting into a bath—after you get used to it, it ain't so hot!*

Chapter 11

The Divorce

When I married Estelle, I knew the statistics. The odds were fifty-fifty that our marriage was going to fail. So I hedged my bet. I filled out the marriage certificate in *disappearing* ink.

On our honeymoon night, I told Estelle I wanted to go out and find some champagne and roses. Instead, I went downtown and broke into City Hall. I went to the marriage records bureau, found our file, ripped it up, and set it on fire in the wastebasket. *Then* I went on my honeymoon.

Five years later the marriage disintegrated. We had grown to loathe each other. The inevitable proclamation finally came:

"I'm suing you for divorce and I'm going to take everything you have," said Estelle. "You hear me? *Everything!* I'm going for the throat!"

The next thing I knew, a process server appeared at the door and handed me a copy of Estelle's divorce petition.

And They Ask Me Why I Drink?

I took it to my lawyer. When he had finished reading it, he said, "Whew! It looks like Estelle's trying to really stick it to you!"

"Not to worry." I laughed. "There's no record of the marriage!"

"What?"

"There's no record of the marriage," I repeated. "So you write her lawyer and tell him our position is that Estelle and I were never married. We just knew each other very, very well. In fact, maybe not so well at all. Yeah, that's it. We were just acquaintances—passing acquaintances."

When Estelle's attorney received that letter, he flipped out and immediately called my lawyer. "What do you mean they were never married?" he said angrily. "If he wants to play that game, he's in for a lot of trouble!"

The next day Estelle's attorney went down to City Hall to get a copy of the marriage license, but, of course, it no longer existed. When he told Estelle he'd been unable to find any record of our betrothal, she exploded.

"Well, we were married!" she shouted, pounding the desk for emphasis. "There were people there, by God."

But the attorney explained to Estelle that since no marriage license existed, she would need documentation. "How about photographs?" she asked. "We've got tons of pictures of Nino and me together!"

"Not good enough," the attorney said. "A lot of people take pictures when they're living together."

"Well, what about the wedding photos?" she cried.

The attorney shook his head. "That won't work, either. A lot of people attend parties," he explained.

Estelle was beside herself with aggravation and for a while I actually believed I was going to get off scot-free.

I was in the proverbial catbird seat until we finally appeared in divorce court. Her lawyer looked at me slyly. "If it pleases the court," he said, "I'd like to present exhibit A. The defendant, Nino Grease Mannelli, claims not only that he and my client were not married, but that he only had a passing acquaintance with this woman. But look at this, Your Honor—it's a piece of gum that he left in her navel on the way down!"

Everyone in the courtroom gasped. "Furthermore," the lawyer added, "we have had the saliva tested, and DNA analysis reveals that there is absolutely no question as to whose mouth this saliva came from!"

The divorce was final and Estelle stalked away from the courthouse. I felt relieved, certain that we would never want to see each other again. But after only a couple of weeks, Estelle called.

"How are you?" she asked, ever so sweetly.

"Fine," I replied, astonished.

"So," she said, "we're divorced. That means there's no reason to hold anything back from me. Is there something you'd like to tell me?"

"Well, let's see. The dog isn't eating too well since you've been gone."

"No," she interrupted. "I mean is there anything you'd like to tell me about love, about discovery, about passion?"

"Let me get my thoughts together, Estelle. I haven't been with anybody since the divorce."

"Well, I have!" she said smugly.

"It's only been two weeks and you're already having an affair with someone?!"

"Actually, it's not some*one*," she replied. "I've had affairs with a photographer, a gardener, and this businessman who was in town for the weekend. I've had sex with a married man, and there was this ex-boxer, and then I had a fling with a young college kid and . . ."

"My God," I interjected, "that's a lot of action in two weeks, Estelle!"

"I'm just trying to discover the meaning of life!"

"I understand," I replied, "but it certainly isn't written on somebody's hydraulics!"

After the divorce and that phone call, I was so depressed I just couldn't see straight. If the Golden Gate Bridge had been in close proximity, I would have jumped. I decided to take a trip. I wanted to go someplace where I knew I wouldn't run into anyone who would ask, "Hey, Nino, how are you doing? How's Estelle?"

A couple of my buddies suggested we all go to Tijuana for the weekend. Why not? I thought.

The guys were all excited at the prospects Tijuana held for an unforgettable weekend. They've got signs down there that flash "WOMEN! WOMEN! WOMEN!" Those girls will do anything you want! You pay the price and they're yours! As my pals pointed out, "Nothing cures a broken heart better than a good snarlin'!" We piled in the car and drove south of the border.

When we got to Tijuana, we found a tawdry place. A guy leaning against the bar was picking his teeth. *"Señor Gringo,"* he said, "anything you want we have here. Ingus, hobble-de-goe, bobble-de-gee, wobble-de-gee. Whatever you want, we got it."

"C'mon," the guys said. "You need a good romp!" They pushed me inside a room, where the madam grabbed me.

"Okay, my little *gringito,*" she said, "you go into Room Three and Carmelita will show you a good time."

Pretty soon Carmelita arrived. She was a little rough for

my tastes. I kind of embraced her, but finally I just walked out of the room.

"Here's the money," I said to the madam. "I can't go through with it."

I ran out into the street. The guys, who'd been watching through the keyhole, followed me.

"I appreciate what you guys are doing," I told them, "but I just can't zap that woman."

"Why not?" they asked. "Was it because you were thinking about those thirty-five guys she probably had earlier today?"

I shook my head no.

"Was it because she hadn't had a bath in three weeks?"

"No."

"Was it the boils on her butt?"

"No!" I shouted. "I just couldn't stand the garlic on her *breath!*"

Of course, I dated a lot of women in the years following my divorce from Estelle. The first one of them was pretty special. God, was she *schweet!* Knowing that I was still bruised from the breakup, she tenderly took me by the hand and led me through all the steps of love.

In the aftermath of our ingus, she lay with her head on my powerful, broad chest, playing with my doodads.

"That's odd!" she said.

"What's odd?"

"I only feel one doodad!" she replied.

"I only have one doodad," I explained.

"How come?" she asked. "Were you sick? Was it an accident?"

"Neither. Like I told you, in the divorce Estelle got *half of everything!*"

* * *

And They Ask Me Why I Drink?

Yes, Estelle got half of everything. At least I didn't have to make any alimony payments. It was, as the pundits say, a clean split.

I've got friends who weren't that fortunate. Ten years later, they're still paying off their first wives. One friend of mine called his ex-wife's office not long ago to see if she'd received her monthly alimony check.

The phone rang and rang. Finally, an unfamiliar voice answered. "Hi," my friend said. "Is June there?"

After a pause, the voice said, "I guess you haven't heard the bad news. June was killed last week in an automobile accident."

Ten minutes later, my friend dialed that number again. And again this same voice answered.

"May I speak to June, please?"

"Hey, I recognize your voice! I just told you, June was killed in a car accident! She's dead."

Fifteen minutes later, my friend called back a third time. "Could I speak to June, please?"

"*It's you again?* What are you, some kind of nut?"

"No," my friend explained. "I just like hearing the 'June is dead' part so much, I can't stop dialing this number!"

I think it should be mandatory to stay single for at least five years after you get divorced. My divorce from Estelle was so bad I just wanted to go into seclusion and get away from all women. Don't get me wrong—I hadn't turned into a woman-hater. But having gone through a brutal divorce, the last thing I wanted was another marriage.

My divorce unexpectedly brought up anxieties that I would never procreate, that the Mannelli seed would wither and die unplanted, that no little Ninos would romp through this world.

I couldn't allow that to happen.

Turned off as I was by women at that point, I decided that I would have a child without becoming romantically entangled. In fact, I would achieve this without even becoming *physically* entangled.

I decided to become a sperm donor. I would live on. The kid wouldn't know me and I wouldn't know him— but at least I would have the satisfaction of knowing I wasn't the end of the genetic line for the Oscar Grease Mannelli family.

I let my fingers do the walking and found a sperm bank not far from home. I walked in and the doctor recorded my medical history. "Mr. Mannelli," he said, "we'd be proud to have you donate. Step right into that room, and a nurse will assist you."

Following the doctor's orders, I walked into the room where a fetching young nurse was waiting for me. Attired in my tank top and shorts, I couldn't help but feel bold. When she asked if I needed some assistance, I had only one response. "Absolutely!"

An hour later, soaked with sweat, I emerged from the room with my little vial. "Here you go, Doc!"

"Well," he said, "it's about time, Mr. Mannelli! What took you so long?"

"It really didn't take *me* so long, Doc." I laughed. "I spent most of the time trying to get the nurse to *cough it back up!*"

Part III

My Many, Many Hats

CALLER: *I spent a little time in the hospital recently, and I'm still having nightmares about this one particular nurse. I'm telling you, Grease, she would make a drill sergeant seem like a pussycat! Did you ever run into one of those tough gals during your medical career?*

GREASEMAN: *Funny you should mention that, because I was just thinking about this wise-ass nurse I used to work with. One day, I cornered her in the hallway of the hospital. "Nurse Cumbubble!" I screamed. "The patient in room thirty-two has diarrhea. Why isn't it on his chart?" "Because," she said, "I got most of it in the pan!"*

Chapter 12

Career Moves, Part 1: Medicine Man

Though radio was always my true love, it wasn't my only career. In fact, I had several careers before I turned to radio.

My convoluted tale begins right after my college days, with my enrollment in Harvard Medical School. While at Harvard, I did a rotation in the psych ward of a nearby hospital. One of the patients thought that he was the King of Prussia. Every single day he would march up and down the hallway, expecting everyone to bow to him. I spent months trying to convince him he wasn't the King of Prussia. One day I was on duty when they brought in another guy in a straitjacket. "What's your problem?" I asked.

" 'My problem' is that I'm the King of Prussia," he answered. "These people don't recognize me!"

I didn't say a thing. Instead, the minute the guy was led off to his padded cell, I got on the phone to the hospital administrator. "You'll never believe this," I told the boss, "but we've got another King of Prussia!"

"What?"

"You heard me right. We've got *another* guy who thinks he's the King of Prussia!"

"Why don't we put these two guys in the same room?" I suggested. "Maybe then they'll realize they both can't be the King of Prussia. It'll help them!"

"Good thinking," he said. "Go ahead and arrange for them to become roommates."

I worked it out so that the two Prussian kings would share a room. I couldn't wait to get to work the next morning. I was running up the stairs to my office the next day when I ran smack dab into our first King of Prussia. "So," I inquired, "how was your night?"

"It was great!" he said. "I found out I'm not the King of Prussia!"

"No kidding? That's fantastic!"

The guy smiled and nodded. "Yes," he said, "it was fantastic! I found out I'm the *Queen* of Prussia!"

That place was a real loony bin. Patients had every kind of neurosis and psychosis. One day Mr. Douglas, a long-term resident, saved another patient from a suicide attempt in the bathtub. After learning of this heroic act, I called Mr. Douglas to my office.

"Mr. Douglas," I said, "you've been in this institution for twenty years now. After reviewing your medical records, we believe you no longer need this institution and its constraints. We think you are rehabilitated, and ready to rejoin society."

"Thank you," Mr. Douglas said.

"By the way," I continued, "I see on our record here that you saved a man from committing suicide in a bathtub. I wish I could tell you he's still around but, unfortunately, he killed himself only a few hours later with a rope."

Mr. Douglas looked at me oddly. "Oh, no," he calmly explained, "he didn't kill himself! *I hung him up to dry!*"

I began my career as a physician by interning in the emergency room of a large hospital. It was quite a learning experience.

Walking into the ER waiting room one morning, I smelled a hideous odor. I immediately realized that someone had taken a clandestine massive. I looked at the people sitting there. "Did somebody take a massive in their britches?" I inquired.

Everyone averted their eyes and looked down at the floor.

"You might as well come clean," I said, "because I'm going to find out who did it."

I questioned every person in that waiting room. Then I saw a drunk slumped in a corner chair. Aha! As I moved closer to him the odor became increasingly unbearable. I had to stop about three feet away from him.

"How come you didn't answer when I asked who had taken a massive in their pants?" I asked.

"Well," he mumbled, "you didn't ask if it was *today!*"

This one old geezer showed up one afternoon in the ER. He'd been bitten by a raccoon.

"This isn't a serious bite," I told him, "but since we don't have the raccoon that bit you, we don't know whether or not it has rabies. Wouldn't matter anyway," I added, "because we're out of the rabies serum."

"My God," he cried, "what should I do?"

"If I were you, old-timer, I'd make believe that raccoon did have rabies and I'd start writing my last will and testament!"

The guy grabbed a pencil and some paper off the counter and frantically began writing. Ten minutes later, he was still at it.

My curiosity got the better of me. "Pop," I said, "what in the hell do you own? That's an awfully long will."

He looked at me and gave an ugly laugh. "This ain't a will," he said. "It's a list of all the people *I'm going to bite!*"

I think the most difficult part of being a doctor is delivering bad news to patients. I didn't like dealing with weeping next-of-kin. I was never comfortable being around grief and hysteria.

One of my patients died on the operating table, and the family was waiting outside the operating room in the hallway. Instead of facing them, I just stuck my arm out the operating room door, and gave them the old thumbs down.

That was when old Dr. Glasnos decided to speak to me about my bedside manner. "You've got to sugarcoat it," he explained. "You've got to give them a little bit of the good with the bad."

When I left his office, I was determined to completely overhaul my presentation. I got the opportunity several days later when an elderly man sat in my office, quaking with fear.

I could tell he was expecting bad news by the way he looked at me when I entered the room. So instead of sitting behind my desk, I sat down in the chair beside him.

"I've gone over all the tests," I told him, "and I've got same good news for you and some bad news."

"Give me the good news first."

"The good news is that your condition can be completely cured with a transplant."

His face brightened and the anxiety disappeared. "Why, that's fantastic," he cried. "What's the bad news?"

"The bad news," I said slowly, "is that they don't make that part anymore!"

I eventually developed a certain flair for delivering news to my patients, even under the worst of circumstances.

I operated on this man with prostate cancer. It was a very difficult operation. *Very* complicated. It wasn't until the last stitch had been sewn that I realized I had made a horrible mistake.

I waited in the recovery room until the patient came out of the anesthesia. "Sir," I began, "I have some bad news and some good news about your operation. While I was operating on your prostate, my hand slipped during the surgery. I accidentally cut off your *doodads*."

He looked at me in stunned silence.

"My God," he said, pulling himself up on his elbows, "what could be the good news?"

I patted him gently on the shoulder. "The good news," I said, "is they're not malignant!"

After that fiasco, the hospital decided that it would be a good idea for me to enter private practice. I hung out my shingle: "Dr. Grease Mannelli, Groinecologist." I hired a nurse and added my name to the Yellow Pages.

On my first day as a private practitioner I had a patient named Mrs. Oppengroid. I blanched as I threw the speculum to the cat for one last survey of her female organs.

"It looks like everything is all right," I told her. She tossed off the sheet and sat up on the examining table.

"However," I added, "when you have a couple of free days I'd like to excise some of those stalagmites I see up in there."

"Fine," she said, "but in the meantime, Doctor, I wonder . . . Could you examine my son? He's been incorrigible lately, and I think it's medically related. He's fourteen years old, and I think his hormones are going wild."

"All right," I said, "I'll talk to the boy."

She left the office and a few seconds later the kid walked in. His mother was right—he was surly.

"What do you want, sawbones?" he asked. "There's nothing wrong with me. I feel great."

"A little exam just to make sure you're on top of your game won't hurt. Take off your clothes and put this little robe on. We'll see what the deal is."

A few minutes later, the boy was sitting on the edge of the examining table. Disgust was written all over his puberty-pocked face. I checked under his tongue, looked in his ears, and checked his eyes. "Your mother tells me you haven't been yourself lately," I said, watching his pupils dilate from the beam of light.

"Well," he admitted, "I really don't feel too good down below."

"All right," I said, "turn around on the table and get up on all fours. Let's have a look."

As he did so, I looked and saw what appeared to be a fuzzy paw protruding from his *bombays!*

"Son," I said, "I think I've located the problem. Grab the sides of the table and hold on!"

I got hold of that piece of fur and I yanked and pulled. The paw turned into a leg which turned into a head which turned into . . . a rabbit!

"Okay, son, you can get dressed now." I put the rabbit down on the floor. While the boy was dressing and the rabbit was hopping, I stepped outside to talk to the boy's mother.

She stood up, an anxious look on her face. "Doctor," she said, "did you find out what the problem was?"

"I certainly did, Mrs. Oppengroid. Your son had a *wild hare up his ass!*"

Despite my great knowledge of medicine, I have to confess I never understood people. I understood what made them sick but I never understood what made them tick.

One family I encountered was extremely poor. The youngest boy was in desperate need of a heart transplant. The family couldn't afford the complex procedure or the postoperative care necessary to save the child.

One day the child's mother heard about a cable TV program that would pay for medical operations. In return, the show was allowed to do a live telecast of the procedure.

The woman immediately telephoned the network and told them about her child. The network producers were all excited. "A live heart transplant, and a kid too. It's sure to be a ratings winner!"

The network arranged the operation and got the necessary clearance to telecast live, coast to coast. The producers even found a donor.

At the scheduled hour, the nurses wheeled the child into the operating room. With the cable cameras capturing the entire procedure from every possible angle, the operation began. Halfway through the operation, complications developed. The child died, right on the operating table on live TV.

Not wanting to miss a moment of this real-life drama, the camera crew raced into the waiting room where the mother was sitting. They put a camera on her and zoomed in for a close-up.

"Hi, everybody!" the woman said, smiling and waving into the camera. "Hi, Joe! Hi, Mom! Hi, Junior! How are you all doing?"

She turned to the cameraman and asked, "Is it okay if I say hello to our neighbors, too?"

The cameraman nodded yes, though he was in total shock. The mother continued to chatter, greeting all her neighbors.

After the telecast was finished, the cameraman went up to the woman.

"Lady," he said, "you're pretty cheerful, considering your child died just an hour ago!"

"Hey," she replied with a big smile, "that's *show business!*"

This guy came to my office and said, "Doc, I've got a sexual problem."

"What kind of problem?" I asked.

"It's a little weird," he replied. "When I stick it in, my vision gets blurred, and when I stick it in all the way, I can't see a thing!"

"That *is* weird! You better let me take a look."

Imagine my shock and surprise when the guy *stuck out his tongue!*

One of my patients was a pregnant young woman. She had dated so many guys she didn't have a clue as to which one was the baby's father. She decided she was still going to have the baby, regardless of its dubious parentage.

When she came in for her weekly checkup, she confessed she was embarrassed at not knowing whose name to put on the upcoming birth certificate.

"Don't worry," I told her. "The main thing is that the baby is healthy."

I took some X-rays of her womb, and gave her a sonogram. "Hmmm," I told her, "the baby looks like it might have sort of a swarthy complexion. Have you ever dated any Middle Eastern guys?"

"Yeah," she said, "a bunch of Israelis! I find those people to be very beautiful."

"Wow, look at this!" I said. "The baby's got straight jet black hair! Have you ever dated any Native Americans?"

"Yes," she admitted. "Apaches and Navajos. With their proud heritage I just couldn't resist."

I studied the X-ray further. "The baby's got either blue or green eyes. Dated any Nordic guys?"

"Yeah. Swedes, Danes, and Finlanders."

"Well," I said, "you've had a very varied love life, indeed."

She was silent for a moment. "Doctor Mannelli," she

finally said. "Let me be honest with you. I'll be happy if this baby doesn't come out *barking!*"

When I started out in medicine I had high ideals, big expectations, and huge dreams. I dreamed about finding a cure for cancer or for AIDS. I yearned to go down in history with the likes of Jonas Salk, Christian Barnard, and Madame Curie. In time, though, I realized that what I really wanted was a Maserati. That meant getting those patients in and out of my office as quickly as possible.

I decided to abandon my groinecology practice and become a general practitioner, operating the world's first drive-in doctor's office. No longer would patients have to get out of the car with their coughs, colds, and colic. Instead, they could wait in line in air-conditioned comfort. It was safer for them and it was better for me, since I would be on the other side of a glass, far from their streptococci.

The patients would pull up and, just like a bank teller, I'd lean into the microphone. "What's your problem?" I'd ask.

The patient might say, "It's a bad case of nausea!"

I'd write out a quick prescription for Compozine and slide it over to them. "Take a couple of these. If you're still nauseated tomorrow, drive by and I'll take another look at you."

Patients might stop because of a nervous condition. I'd write out a prescription for Valium.

They might drive up with a cold. "Come over here to the glass," I'd say. "Stick out your tongue and say aaahh . . . Oh, you've got a strep throat. Here's a prescription for penicillin. Stay home and rest in bed."

I'd get a patient in and out of there in ten minutes at fifty dollars a pop.

Everything was going great until I misdiagnosed two cases of Rocky Mountain spotted fever because the window was dirty. The two patients died and then the newspapers got hold of the story. I had no choice but to abandon the drive-in, even though it was still financially lucrative. The next day's headlines proclaimed me: "Quack in the Box!"

After the drive-in practice, I switched specialties once again and became Dr. Grease Mannelli, psychiatrist!

I'll never forget the most tragic case I ever had to deal with. It involved a woman who came to me because of her physical unattractiveness. Actually, between you and me, she was repulsive. Okay, there's absolutely no way around it—she was just flat-assed ugly!

Her ugliness caused her trouble in every area of her life. She couldn't land a date, or a job, and she didn't have the money for plastic surgery.

So she did the next best thing. She made an appointment with me.

I conducted a preappointment interview with the woman over the phone. She believed she was borderline insane because she was so ugly. She despaired of anyone ever seeing the gentle soul that awaited beneath her hideous surface.

I was so moved by our telephone conversation that I insisted she come to my office immediately.

When the woman arrived, I greeted her warmly, but I have to admit that I found her homely, almost beyond belief. Still, I was determined not to reveal my discomfort.

"I feel your depression, loneliness, and sadness," I said. "I'm going to try my very best to help you overcome these feelings of unworthiness."

"Oh, Doctor," she said. "Do you really think you can help me?"

"Absolutely," I said. "So let's get started."

"Great!"

"Go over to the couch," I said, "and if you would . . . lie *facedown!*"

CALLER: *What was it like looking in all those mouths, Grease, back in your dentist days? I mean, did you ever find anything disgusting?*

GREASEMAN: *One day, I was examining this guy's yap and said, "Ah, I see you've been doing some carpet munching." He smiled. "How'd ya know, Doc? Find a hair in my teeth?" "No," I replied, "you've got a poop smudge on your chin."*

Chapter 13

Career Moves, Part 2: Dentist

People think being a doctor is exciting, but it usually isn't. For the most part, every day resembles the one before, with the same parade of diseases, the same petty complaints, hour after hour. You're forced to feign concern when you're really thinking about your golf game.

I decided to make a career change. Kind of a lateral move, you might say. I became a dentist.

My interest in dentistry started because of my joyful appreciation of nitrous oxide. I'd go to the dentist, sit down in the chair, and shout, "Nitrous! Give me nitrous!"

The dental hygienist would smile and turn that thing on high; then nothing would bother me. She could've run the drill on my *bombays* and it wouldn't have troubled me.

The one thing I did notice, however, was that the

nitrous vastly increased my sense of taste. I realized that the first time the hygienist was working on me. My head was back and she had her hands in my mouth.

"Hey," I said. "I'm tasting onions!"

She smiled. "That's a pretty good set of taste buds you have," she said. "As a matter of fact, I had liver and onions for lunch today, Mr. Mannelli."

I had another appointment a couple of months later. The hygienist was cleaning my teeth. "Hmm," I said, "you had a pepperoni pizza for lunch today, didn't you?"

"That's right," she said. "We were so rushed we ordered in pizza today."

Three months later, I was back for another cleaning. The hygienist stuck her fingers in my mouth. The taste was so horrible, so hideous, I started to gag. Still, she continued with the cleaning.

"You can lean forward and spit now," she said when she was finished.

I leaned forward, all right, but I didn't spit. I threw up!

"You must be having a bad reaction to the nitrous!" she said. "Just sit quietly for a moment."

I was lying in the chair, sweat pouring down my face, trying to control the nausea. I couldn't understand what had happened until, to my horror, I heard her speaking to the dentist. "By the way, Dr. Mike," she said, "we're out of toilet paper in the bathroom."

Maybe those rubber gloves the hygienists wear aren't such a bad thing after all.

I was cleaning out a closet recently when I found my old diploma from dental school. I don't like to remember that time in my life because, truth to tell, I was a lousy dentist. My patients called me Dr. Mannelli, but to my coworkers I was The Butcher of Bayonne.

Career Moves, Part 2: Dentist

To be a dentist you have to be both learned and skilled. I was learned, but I wasn't exactly skilled with my hands. I was simply not adept at the craftsmanship associated with dentistry.

It was terrible. I just couldn't get the procedures down. I'd be drilling away and suddenly I think, "What did I forget?" Then I'd hear a scream and remember: "Oh, yeah, the Novocain." I just couldn't keep my mind on my business.

One time, I had a new patient in the chair. She was a very attractive lady, who evidently found the doctor simply irresistible. She deliberately pressed her body into mine. She leaned over to spit into the basin and purposely displayed her ample Eldridge Cleavage. As I leaned forward to begin working on her cavity, she poked me with her knee, looked deep into my eyes, and said, "Na-na-Nooky!"

"Well," I smiled, "that's just the sort of cavity I was hoping to fill!"

That was the beginning of the end of my practice. After that initial ingus and sweet Shangri-la, I'd always make sure when she came to see me that she was the last patient of the day. Man, it was *schweet!*

I'd tell my hygienist she could leave, adjust the chair, and . . . "Who's your dentist? Who's your dentist? Who's your dentist?"

The woman couldn't get enough of me, and kept making appointments. Finally I said, "We'd better knock this off. You're married, and your husband is bound to be getting suspicious."

"Why should he be suspicious?" she asked. "We've been doing this for six months and he hasn't asked me any questions."

And They Ask Me Why I Drink?

"Yeah," I said, "but he will soon! You're down to *one tooth!*"

I had one final contribution to make to the dental profession before I put away my drill forever. It's an anthem for dentists everywhere. I call it "The Dentist Rap," and it goes like this:

Why are your teeth out of whack?
Could they be covered in unsavory plaque?
Twisted molars, bicuspids awry,
Don't get pyorrhea in my eye!

Let's rap, rap, do the dentist's rap.

The other day a long-lost pal,
came to see me for a root canal.
He hurt so bad he could hardly see—
the poor man was in a-go-ny!
I said "Oh my God, you must be in pain,
you hardly noticed the Novocain!"

Rap, rap, it's the dentist's rap!

So the next time you eat a candy bar,
crash through the windshield of your car;
The next time on a Saturday night,
you get yourself in a barroom fight;
The next time you play hockey without protection,
or have yourself an untreated infection;
I ain't gonna begin to bitch,
'cause all those things are making me rich!
Doing the work, no pain you'll feel!
Paying the bill, that's when you'll squeal!

Rap, rap, it's the dentist's rap.

CALLER: *Grease, I'm just getting out of law school. Any advice?*

GREASEMAN: *Just remember the most important thing when practicing law: The large print giveth, and the small print taketh away.*

Chapter 14

Career Moves, Part 3: Attorney at Law

After I left dentistry, I decided to pursue another interest: law. I took a thirty-day mail order course and got my degree. I rented an office and hung out my shingle: "Grease Mannelli, Attorney."

I once acted as the prosecuting attorney against a sleazy exhibitionist, a man caught wagging his hydraulics at a woman on the bus. He was conferring with his attorney when the jurors, many of whom were young, lovely women, were ushered into court.

Faced with this attractive, attentive audience, the defendant apparently couldn't help himself. No sooner was the jury seated than he jumped up on the defense table and dropped his pants. In full view of the jury, he began wailing away!

One of the women jurors turned to the judge. "Isn't that illegal?" she screamed.

And They Ask Me Why I Drink?

Before the judge could answer, I spoke up. "You're darn tootin' it's illegal! *He's getting fingerprints all over exhibit A!*"

A murder case I handled still sticks out vividly in my mind.

I was seated at the defense table when the prosecuting attorney called his star witness. Man, was she *schweet!* She had a bodacious set of ta-tas and a turd cutter that would make a bishop kick in a stained-glass window!

She was sworn in and sat down in the witness box.

"Madam," the prosecutor said, "will you please tell us where you were Monday night."

"I was with my boyfriend."

"And where were you on Tuesday night?"

"I was with my other boyfriend."

The prosecutor approached the witness stand. "And last night? Can you tell us where you were last night?"

"Certainly," she said with a smile. "I spent the night with *another* boyfriend."

The prosecutor gave her a long look. "Can I ask you what you're going to be doing on Thursday night?"

At that point, I pounded on the table. "Objection, your honor! I asked her *first!*"

I handled a paternity case once where I represented a woman who was suing her ex-boyfriend. I was in the middle of cross-examining the fellow intently when the guy looked up at the judge. "Your Honor," he said, "I think we can bring this case to a quick conclusion. I can't be the father of this woman's child. I have in my hand the actual condom I wore on the night we had intercourse."

He pulled a condom out of his pocket and dangled it in front of the jury.

"Let me see that condom, sir!" I demanded. I grabbed it out of his hand and unrolled it to full length. I walked over to the judge's personal carafe of water, and filled the condom. As I suspected, it leaked like a sieve!

I held the dripping condom in front of the jury, then spun around to the defendant. "I'm sorry, sir, but your alibi just *doesn't hold water!*"

I was doing quite well as an attorney until I decided to join a large law firm. The trouble started when the firm hired a new receptionist. God, was she great looking!

I had fantasies about her until I discovered one of the lawyers was putting the stones to her. At that point I decided it was hands off. It was a smart decision. I later learned the senior partner had called the attorney into his office, and asked if the rumor was true: Was he nailing the receptionist?

The attorney admitted it was true. "She's so wild," he explained, "that making love to my wife feels like making love to a fire hydrant."

The senior partner thanked the guy for his honesty and that was the end of the discussion. A few weeks later, however, the lawyer entered the senior partner's office.

"Can I ask *you* a personal question?" the attorney said.

"Sure," the senior partner said. "Close the door. What is it?"

"I heard a rumor that *you* are noodling the new receptionist too. Is it true?"

The senior partner smiled. "Yes," he said, "as a matter of fact I am. And I have to agree with you. Making love to her is special, and *making love to your wife is like making love to a fire hydrant!*"

CALLER: *Hey, Grease, I got a job in radio. I'm going to be a salesman. Any advice?*
GREASEMAN: *Sure. Dress British and think Yiddish.*

Chapter 15

Career Moves, Part 4: Advertising Man

After learning the ins and outs of the law, I decided to try something new. I decided to try the advertising game.

In no time at all, I was a hotshot copywriter. And then Daddy chose to pay me a visit at work.

"I'm out on the loading docks," Daddy said, "busting my chops, and making chump change. You sit behind your big desk, sell air, and make a fortune. I had to come up to see how it's done."

Daddy's visit coincided with an important board meeting. The entire staff was called together to discuss the firm's new condom account. Since it had just become legal to advertise condoms on the radio, the account spelled big bucks for the agency. We were all sitting around the conference room table, trying to come up with an advertising campaign.

"I think we should emphasize the safety factor involved in protected lovemaking," an executive said. "Something along the line of, 'If you really care, safety you'll share!'"

Someone else suggested, "Dispense latex in love!"

All of a sudden, Daddy interrupted. "You all don't know anything, do you? I can't believe you're talking about selling condoms with slogans like that. I may not wear a fancy suit, but I can sure as hell come up with better ideas than you guys.

"For instance," continued Daddy, "how about this one? 'Cover your stump before you hump!' Or 'Don't be silly, protect your willie!'"

"Daddy!" I whispered. "That's enough! Be quiet!"

Daddy brushed me aside. "Why," he said, "I could come up with these all day long. 'If you're not gonna sack it, go home and whack it!' 'If you think she's spunky, shield your monkey!'"

"Daddy," I begged. "Will you please shut up! You're gonna cost me my job!"

"Cost you?" he cried. "I'm trying to *save* your job!"

He just kept on going. " 'If he's between those thighs, he should be condomized!' 'If you go into heat, package your meat!'"

I couldn't stand it anymore. "I'm very sorry, everyone," I said, standing up. "This is my father. I brought him to this meeting, but I had no idea he was going to interrupt us with these idiot slogans. If you'll excuse us . . ."

I hauled Daddy out of his chair and steered him toward the door. He was still spouting slogans as we exited the conference room. " 'When you take off her pants and blouse, suit up and cover your mouse!'"

I smacked Daddy. "Be quiet!"

"You can't shut me up!" he said in a booming voice, and just kept on blabbering. " 'Especially in December, gift wrap that member!'

" 'Don't be a fool, organize that tool!'"

And They Ask Me Why I Drink?

" 'Wrap it in foil before you check her oil!' "

Everyone sat stunned as I dragged Daddy out of the room and to the elevator.

Even as the elevator descended, I could still hear old Daddy yelling: " *'Wrap it in rubber before you shove it in her blubber!'* "

CALLER: *Greaseman, what was the most brutal force you used to bring a maggot in when you were a lawman?*

GREASEMAN: *Well, one time I had three suspects and only two pairs of handcuffs. So I cuffed two of the suspects and stuck them in the backseat of the patrol car. Then I slammed the third suspect's long hair in the car door and made him jog alongside to the station.*

Chapter 16

Career Moves, Part 5: Lawman

After Daddy destroyed my advertising career, I decided to move on to something more exciting. With my law background, a natural move for me was to law enforcement. Legal training aside, I wanted to know what it was like to strap on a gun, pin on a badge, and go after society's bad guys.

I got a job as deputy sheriff. Soon I was sitting behind the wheel of a black-and-white patrol car, complete with siren, police radio, and flashing lights.

Some people get turned on listening to Beethoven. Nothing turned me on more than listening to my police radio, and responding that I was "10-51 to the scene." It was exciting being out on patrol. You never knew what was going to happen next.

One night I was out cruising. I was late for my appointment with Gagging Annie and my hemmies were burning something fierce. To make matters worse, the Bavarian cream pie I'd had for dessert was giving me a terrible case of indigestion. I was not in a mood to take anybody's crap.

I came up over a hill and suddenly had to hit my brakes. A long line of cars and trucks were at a dead stop in the middle of nowhere.

I turned on the lights and got out of the patrol car to see what the problem was.

When I got to the front of the line of backed-up traffic, I saw an abandoned auto in the midst of the highway. A note was tucked under the windshield wiper. I ripped it off. "To whom it may concern, I'm going for help," the note said. "I'll be back in a second."

What an idiot! I climbed up on the roof of the car. "Ladies and gentlemen!" I yelled. "Never leave a car unattended like this! You never know when a bunch of thugs will show up and kick in the headlights!"

I jumped down from the roof and broke both of the headlights with my flashlight.

"Or they might break your car windows and steal your radio!" I walked around the car punching out the windows with the flashlight. The people in the other cars cheered.

I ripped the shirt right off my back, rolled it up, and stuffed it in the gas tank. Then I lit it.

A second later, there was an earth-shaking explosion. The car flew into the air and landed on the shoulder of the road. It was instantly consumed by flames.

I turned to the crowd.

"Now that's where you're supposed to abandon a car," I shouted to the crowd. *"On the shoulder, not in the middle of the damn highway!"*

The one thing I hated about being on patrol was having to work Saturday nights. Other guys would be out with their honeys, going to dinner or to the movies, and there I'd be, manning a sobriety checkpoint. I was always in a bad mood on Saturday nights. Sometimes I wound up taking it out on other people.

One Saturday night, when I was stopping traffic at the checkpoint, I saw a guy in a Porsche with his hot-looking girlfriend. For some reason, it really made me mad. I could tell he was upset about being delayed, so I decided to upset him some more.

When he pulled up and rolled down his window, I bent down and belched. Obnoxious fumes from my hideous lunch wafted right in his face.

"How are you tonight, sir?" I asked. "You haven't been drinking, have you?"

The guy looked at me with disdain. "I don't drink. I'm a teetotaler."

"I don't know, sir. I smell something. You'll have to step out of the car. I'm going to have to give you a sobriety test!"

The guy grudgingly got out of the car. I handed him an unwashed breathalyzer mask that some elderly refugee had thrown up in.

"Breathe in here," I said.

Of course, the guy started gagging.

"I'm not getting a reading," I said, "but that doesn't mean you haven't been drinking. Let me hear you recite the alphabet."

He sang his ABCs perfectly.

"All right," I said, "I want you to walk toe-to-heel with your arms out. Then stop and touch your nose."

He did all of this without a problem.

"I think you might just be one of those people who drinks but doesn't show it. A telltale sign, though, is a loss of control of your bodily functions. Step to the side of your car and pull your pants down. I want you to break wind for me, son."

"But, Officer . . ."

"If you can't do it, then I'll know you've been drinking!"

The guy went over to the side of the car and pulled his pants down. But he was so nervous that he ended up taking a huge, hideous massive.

"That's it!" I yelled. "You're under arrest."

"Under arrest?" he cried. "What for?"

I looked at him and grinned. "Son, take a look at that sign posted up there. It says 'No Dumping!'"

I was walking my beat one afternoon, and had just crossed an alleyway when I heard a strange sound: *Splat!*

Following my instincts, I walked down the alley. A body was lying crumpled on top of a large Dumpster.

Figuring the guy had committed suicide, I looked up to see where he had jumped from. There was an open window on the fifth floor. Leaving the crime scene for the detectives, I walked around to the front of the building.

The doorman gave me the guy's apartment number, and I went up.

I rang the doorbell. A weeping young woman answered. "I can't believe he jumped!" she cried. "Oh, why? Why?"

"Ma'am," I said, "can you tell me your relationship to the deceased?"

"He was looking for a live-in housekeeper when I met

him," she answered. "When I showed up for the interview, he said he would pay me two hundred and fifty dollars a week, and there would be no hanky-panky.

"I agreed to those terms and everything was great for about two weeks. Then he came to me and asked if I would work *topless*—still with no hanky-panky—for seven hundred fifty dollars a week. I readily agreed."

I was growing impatient. "And then what happened?"

"About a month later," she continued, "he walked into my room, all embarrassed. He asked if I would work around the house in the nude, for one thousand dollars a week, with no hanky-panky.

"I said I would and I thanked him for the raise. Everything was fine," she said, tears welling up in her eyes, "until this afternoon."

"Well," I said, *"what happened?"*

"He called me into the living room and asked how much I would charge him to live here and work nude *with* hanky-panky. I told him for a setup like that, I'd work for free! The next thing I knew, *he jumped out the window!"*

When I was a patrolman, things were a lot different than they are today—the world was a different place. People weren't left lying in the parks or on the sidewalks, their belongings scattered around them. There was still the Bowery but that was different. That was one street, one block. These days there are bums pushing shopping carts with squeaky wheels from one end of town to the other. It certainly wasn't like that when I was a cop.

Take the time I happened upon a vagrant sitting on a bench.

"C'mon, move along!" I said, prodding him with my nightstick. "You can't sit here. Decent people come to this park to walk their dogs and play with their kids."

"But, Officer," he cried. "I've got a job! I'm working here right now!"

"Oh, yeah? And what kind of job do you have that allows you to sit here on a park bench?"

"See that big old neon sign across the street that says 'Countless women use our products'?"

"I see it. So what?"

"Well," he explained, "my job is to watch that sign. If the 'O' in 'Countless' ever burns out, I'm supposed to run over there and *cut off the juice!*"

One afternoon I was walking down the street, swinging my nightstick, looking for action. As I passed by a clock shop, I glanced in the window, and the woman working behind the counter caught my eye. Boy, was she *schweet!* I stood there, kneading my package, thinking I had to cut me a slice of that.

I noticed a sign in the window—"Rolex! $19.95!"—and knew just what to do.

I walked into the store and bellied up to the counter. "Miss," I said, "I'd like to see that $19.95 Rolex."

She smiled sweetly. "I'm sorry, Officer," she said, "but it's not a real watch. There's nothing inside it. The price of a real Rolex is five thousand dollars and up. We just use that sign to get people inside the shop."

"That's false advertising. I could close this store down. I could fine you one hundred thousand dollars, and incarcerate you for six months."

"Oh my," she cried. "I didn't even think about that! I just thought it was funny to put up that price and then show people this fake! Oh, Officer, please, don't arrest me."

I looked at her and smiled. "I might not arrest you if you'll talk to the judge."

She looked puzzled. "I don't understand."

I walked to the front door and turned the "Open" sign around so it read "Closed."

I turned around to face her. "Well," I said, dropping trou, "let me introduce you to *His Honor!*"

I was working at the station one night when a call came in. "Officer," a woman cried, "you've gotta help us. The neighborhood is being overrun by prostitutes. It's outrageous. These women are even carrying signs now. You've got to come over here right now and do something about it!"

"Calm down!" I said. "I'll handle it personally."

I changed out of my uniform and drove over to the woman's neighborhood. Sure enough, there was a hooker carrying a sign: "Best Snarlin' in Town, $25!"

I parked the car and walked over to her. "Hey," I said, "twenty-five dollars for the best snarlin' in town?"

"That's right!"

"Let me see if what you've got is the real stuff."

We got in the back seat of my car, and she started going to town.

She was in the midst of burying face when I said, "All right, stop already. I'm a cop and you're under arrest!"

She was stunned. "My God, Officer," she cried. "What's the charge? Prostitution? Lewd conduct?"

I looked at her and laughed. "No," I said. *"False advertising!"*

I retired from active police duty when I heard the siren call of show business. Nonetheless, I enjoy hooking up with my law enforcement buddies every once in a while, and indulging in some volunteer policing. In fact, not too long ago I accepted an invitation from a couple of my pals in the LAPD to accompany them on The Great Hollywood Hooker Roundup.

So many hookers were arrested that the booking line at the Hollywood precinct was backed up halfway around the block. As I was walking the line, keeping an eye on the girls, this little old lady went shuffling by. "What are you all standing here for?" she asked one of the hookers.

The hooker was evidently embarrassed to tell the elderly woman she'd been arrested on charges of prostitution. "We're in line because they're giving away free oranges, Grandma."

"Free oranges!" the old lady said. "Wow!" She got in line with the hookers.

Little by little, the line moved along. The hookers were photographed, fingerprinted, fined, and released. Eventually, the little old lady made her way to the startled desk sergeant.

He peered at her over the top of his glasses in disbelief. Here was an eighty-year-old grandmother: shoulders stooped, hair in a little bun, her purse clutched tightly to her sagging chest.

The old woman just smiled.

"Bring them on, sonny! I'll take out my teeth and suck 'em dry!"

Over the years, I've worked with a lot of great cops. But I have to nod my head in the direction of the greatest investigator of them all—Sherlock Holmes.

Though everyone knows something of the legendary detective's exploits, few are aware that Holmes and his faithful sidekick, Dr. Watson, liked to have a night out when they weren't solving crimes. I learned this from one of Sherlock's grandchildren, Shylock, with whom I once had the pleasure of dining.

On one occasion Sherlock and Watson went to a concert hall, where they were both entranced by the beautiful young singer. She was a great flirt, dancing about the stage, exhibiting more than a bit of thigh. She sang some bawdy tunes, and when she was finished, Holmes and Watson stood and cheered.

After the concert, the two stopped at a pub and had a brandy. They returned to Holmes's study and resumed pondering a seemingly indecipherable case for Scotland Yard. They'd both been pacing and deliberating for about an hour when suddenly Holmes turned to Watson.

"Stop thinking about that girl!" Holmes said.

Watson was stunned.

"Good God, sir," he said, "how could you possibly have known what I was thinking?"

Holmes smiled slyly. "Elementary, my dear Watson, elementary. First of all, for the past hour you've been pacing back and forth like a bull in heat. You've been humming the tunes she sang with a silly smile on your face. But my deduction really only required one clue—you've absentmindedly *hung* your umbrella on that *bulge* in your *pants!*"

CALLER: *Listen, Grease, have you ever been to a séance, in order to contact the spirits of your past lives?*

GREASEMAN: *No, but one time I visited a* schweet *fortune-teller who told me I would come into some money. And sure enough, I splattered all the change in my pocket!*

Chapter 17

My Past Lives

You'll probably think I'm nuts, mad as a hatter, but I've lived before. My soul has taken other forms, inhabited other bodies.

What we were before, we might be again. In my case, several of my previous lives steered me to my law enforcement career.

I lived as the first Yiddish lawman in the Old West. They called me Irving Grease Manowitz, and I wore a ten-gallon *yarmulke*. Instead of a badge, I wore a *mezuzah*, and instead of guns, I carried two big jars of *kreplach* in my holster. I had a horse that wouldn't gallop or canter; he *schlepped*. I captured the bad guys not with violence, but with guilt.

One day, as I was *schlepping* out of the Silver Dollar Saloon, one of the townspeople rushed over to me.

"Irving, Irving," he cried, "I think there's an illegal enterprise going on."

"Why are you *hoking* me?" I complained. "Can't you see I'm busy. You with your *fercockta* gripes! This whole town is *meshugga!*"

The fellow looked at me quizzically. "What are you speaking there, Sheriff—Apache?"

I just looked at him and shook my head. "What's the problem?"

"It's Colonel Parker."

"Colonel Parker? What's that *goniff* doing?"

"No one's sure," the fellow said. "We see a lot of men walking in and out of his place. They walk in agitated, but they come out with big smiles on their faces."

"Okay," I told him. "I'll look into it. Now vamoose!"

I stationed myself across the street from Colonel Parker's establishment. Noshing on a bagel, I began my surveillance. That fellow had been right! A man would walk up, whisper to the comely looking wench at a booth, and go inside. Not long after, he'd come out with a smile on his face.

"Sheriff," one of the townsfolk asked after my second day on the watch, "ain't you gonna investigate what's going on in there?"

"Yes!" I said. "Stop being such a *nudge!* Don't *hok* me! I'll check it out in my own time, in my own way!"

On the third day I decided to go in undercover as a customer. "Here," I said to a fellow standing nearby, "hold my *mezuzah.*"

I walked across the street and spoke to the woman at the booth. I went inside. When I emerged into the daylight again, I, too, had a big smile on my face.

Everyone ran over to me. "Sheriff," they asked, "did you find out what's going on in there?"

And They Ask Me Why I Drink?

I looked at them. "I can't reveal the total findings of my investigation," I confided, "but let me just say this: I finally had a showdown with the fastest *gums* in the *West!*"

The Silver Dollar Saloon was one of my favorite hangouts in those bygone days, and not only because of the great wine they served. I also had a romantic interest in one of the women employed there.

I was standing at the bar sipping a Manischewitz when Miss Kitty, the *shiksa* I was *shtupping*, sidled up to me. "Sheriff," she said, "what do you say about us going upstairs?"

"I don't know," I said. "I don't feel right about it. I've got *shpilkes*."

She looked puzzled. "Is that contagious?"

"No," I said. "It's *shpilkes*. *Shpilkes!* I'm uneasy."

"C'mon upstairs and let me check."

We went to her room and closed the door. "I'm nervous about my *schmeckle*," I explained.

"What's that?"

"It's *this!*" I said, dropping trou.

"My goodness," she cried, "I ain't ever seen anything like that, Sheriff! You'd better go down to Doc Carter and have him take a look at it!"

I pulled my pants up and walked on down to Doc Carter's office. "Doc," I said, "you gotta help me. I feel *fermisht*. Here," I said, dropping my pants, "take a look at this."

He took one look and went, "Whew! Irving! I think you've got yourself sick."

"Then give me something," I demanded. "What kind of *fercockta* doctor are you, anyway?"

"I think it's a little out of my purview," he said. "Let me call in a member of my staff, a great Indian medicine man—One Who Dissects Wallets."

The medicine man came in and looked at me. He began mumbling in Indian jargon. After about a minute of this mumbo jumbo, I turned to Doc Carter and asked for a translation.

The doctor just shook his head. "He says he can heal the sick, not *raise the dead!*"

During my years as sheriff, I took it upon myself to convert The Wild West to the kosher way of life. You wouldn't believe the food the *goyim* were eating! Pork rinds, hotdogs, fatback! I got a bad case of the *spilkas,* just smelling the unclean food every time I went into the Silver Dollar Saloon.

I started burying the dishes out in the backyard. When Miss Kitty saw what I was doing, she offered to help. "I'll wash the dishes," she said. "You don't have to hide them."

"I'm not hiding them," I explained. "I'm making them pure again."

I called the townsfolk together. "I'm the sheriff of this *fercockta* town," I announced, "and I hereby declare that everything must be kosher from this day forward. I'm going *meshugga* from your pork rinds and bacon bits!"

The town cleaned up the best it could. Out with the pork rinds, in with the kosher hotdogs. Everything was going smoothly until my deputy went to the Silver Dollar Saloon to report back to me on the town's progress.

One of the girls told him I was upstairs with Miss Kitty, and the deputy followed the trail. Not thinking, he opened the door to Miss Kitty's bedroom without knocking. I was with Miss Kitty, my face buried, feasting on the yeast!

"My God, Sheriff," he cried. "And you're worried about kosher? Look at you!"

"Deputy," I said, wiping my face on the sheet. "Let me tell you something: *Even kosher has its limits!*"

Part IV

The Radio and Beyond

Chapter 18

"Ode of the Greaseman"

(Sung to the tune of "If I Only Had a Brain")

I'm the bulky DJ who has
The most enormous doodads,
You won't believe your eyes!
They're as hard as fordham granite,
I could fertilize the planet,
'Cause they're avocado size!

I tell you all sincerely,
We aren't talking nearly,
A man's bravado lies.
For the truth then of course is,
That they're bigger than a horse's,
'Cause they're avocado size!

And They Ask Me Why I Drink?

Oh I must say that mine
could wail away for hours,
and still retain their powers,
to spurt and fertilize!
And each one is a handful,
and as heavy as an anvil,
'cause they're avocado size!

Oh I can count the times
I slammed them in a drawer.
You can whack them,
with a big old two by four.
I might say "ouch," but nothing more!

I hold them while my darling,
administers a snarlin',
'Cause they'd blacken both her eyes.
If those puppies started swaying,
Doctor bills I would be paying
'Cause they're avocado size!

CALLER: *Greaseman, were you ever a patient in the hospital?*

GREASEMAN: *I had to have surgery once and I remember it well. I was lying on the table, and a Candy Striper came in with a razor and shaving cream to prep me. Man, she foamed me up and then she grabbed the old fuselage and started shaving away.*

I tried to control myself, Lord knows, but feeling those delicate little fingers along that nodule-laden implement got me going and . . . oh, God . . . oh man, oh man!

She recoiled in horror and immediately left the room. However, she returned soon after with a warm towel to clean up the mixture of shaving cream and the residue of my uncontrollable lust.

As she was walking out of the room, she turned to me with a big smile on her face. "Did I do a good job?"

"You did a great *job!" I told her. "I'm only here for a* tonsillectomy, *but I really enjoyed it!"*

Chapter 19

Poked, Prodded, and Shrunk

The life of a Boss Jock is fraught with stress and danger. Working that radio every day, baring your soul, takes its emotional, spiritual, and physical toll.

So it is no surprise that one of the many stipulations in my first Boss Jock contract was that I had to get a physical checkup.

I went to the doctor and had a complete exam. He checked every inch of my body, every orifice, from head to toe.

As I was putting my clothes back on, the doctor said, "You know, you're a very healthy man."

"Bulky," I said. "I work out every day."

"There is more to being healthy than lifting weights. I just got the blood test back. You have tremendously high cholesterol and it also looks to me like you're a little florid. Are you a drinking man?"

"Yeah, Doc," I confessed. "You've got to drink if you're a Boss Jock and you're running around with women. Women need wine, dancing, and dining out at fine restaurants. And right now I'm dating a nineteen-year-old Venus."

"My God! You're a man in your thirties!"

"Doesn't matter," I laughed. "I like younger women!"

"Well, then," he said, "let me check a few other things about your lifestyle. What did you have for breakfast this morning?"

"I had a big donut, and coffee."

"Donut!" he exclaimed. "With your high cholesterol?! What about lunch?"

"Onion rings. I had lunch at this all-you-can-eat place. I went back to the buffet table three times!"

The doctor shook his head. "My God. Fast women, donuts, onion rings—it's going to kill you. I'm going to make a list here of the things that you should avoid."

"Avoid? Wait a minute, Doc. I have a lot on my mind. How am I going to remember your damn list?"

"I'll make it simple, Nino," he said. "Just remember this: *If it's got a hole in it, don't mess with it!*"

That sweet medical tale reminds me of another. I was working at a station in Florida, early on in my career, when one of the all-time biggest hurricanes reared up and threatened to blow us all away. The government issued mandatory evacuation orders, sending all of the towns-people to the high school auditorium.

The Red Cross set up cots and hauled drinking water into that auditorium. The one thing they *didn't* have was a doctor. As luck would have it, a pregnant woman started going into labor. "I think I'm gonna have the baby," she cried.

Fortunately, as a former medical man, I was able to assist. "Push, push!" I told her. "That's it! There you go! The baby is fine!"

I cleaned the baby, wrapped it in swaddling clothes, and put it in the mother's arms. Everyone lined up to get a peek at the newborn child.

All the women were gushing over the child, paying the mother compliments, when a ten-year-old boy walked over. He examined the baby for a minute, then he bent over to the mother. "You'd better say something to that kid, ma'am! You're in for a hell of a life if he jumps into that hole every time the wind blows!"

I'm probably the only Boss Jock in America who must seek therapy once a week. The station executives insist I make these weekly visits. "Grease," they declared, "we have a serious investment in you. We're willing to pay for a checkup from the neck up for you, once a week. All you've got to do is go there."

And They Ask Me Why I Drink?

It's right in my contract: "Grease Mannelli must visit the shrink once a week like clockwork."

At first I was ashamed and angry about that clause. I couldn't figure out what the station executives were so worried about. Did they feel I walked such a mental and emotional tightrope that I needed an on-call shrink to make sure I remained a duck-walking, ditty-bopping daddy with a high degree of lucidity?

Or were they overly uneasy about the obsessional love I have for my bone-dry martinis? If my daily consumption of bone-dries was at the root of their concern, they had nothing to worry about. I don't drink anywhere near as much as my daddy—not that he's the best yardstick in the world by which to measure alcoholism.

I remember the time somebody gave him a fifth of a very rare whiskey down at the local bar. Daddy was really excited 'cause he'd never had that kind of top-shelf whiskey before. He carefully placed the bottle in his pocket and started down the road, hurrying home. He was anxious to get back so he could sit down in the living room, light up a Tiparillo, and begin savoring that whiskey.

Unfortunately for Daddy, he was so excited that he wasn't watching where he was going, and he got hit by a car on his way home. The force of the impact spun him in the air and—BOOM!—Daddy landed facedown on the ground by the side of the road.

Although the driver was pretty shaken up, he jumped out of the car and ran over to where Daddy was lying on the ground to make sure he was okay. Daddy just waved him off.

"I'm all right! Just leave me alone," Daddy shouted angrily. He got to his feet, brushed himself off, and started lumbering toward home. He'd only gone a few feet when he felt something trickling down his leg. Panicked, he lifted his face toward heaven.

"Oh, please God!" he cried. "Let it be *blood!*"

I realize that the station's concern about my mental and emotional well-being is probably nothing more than a subtle safeguard. A potential whitewash, you might say, so that if I *do* go nuts, the executives can look at each other in consolation and say, "We tried to get him help. We weren't totally disinterested in the man's mental instability."

The shrink and I became fairly good friends as the weeks turned into months and the months turned into years. He was just as crazy as I was . . . or am.

A couple of weeks ago, for instance, he told me that he was unable to help me with one of my problems.

"I'm terribly sorry," he said, "but your kleptomania is incurable. I've been working with you for six months, and there has been no significant change in your behavior."

I suddenly dropped the paperweight I'd taken off his desk. "Oh God," I cried, "what am I going to do?"

"Well," the doctor said softly, "next week, on your way here for your appointment, why don't you drive by Johnson Electric and pick me up a new CD player!"

All in all, though, the radio station shrink has done me more good than harm. Just the other day, I had a session with him and said, "You know, I really feel cured! I need to celebrate. Will you kiss me?"

"Kiss you?" he replied. "That would be a total violation of my professional ethics. Hell, I shouldn't even be lying here naked next to you!"

CALLER: *Hey, Grease, I don't know if you're a religious person, but do you have a favorite hymn?*
GREASE: *Actually, I do! It's one I wrote myself:*
> *That bone, that bone, that bone-dry,*
> *That gift from God I swear by!*
> *There ain't no need to ask why,*
> *Just praise the name of the Lord!*

Chapter 20

Me and My Bone-Dry Martinis

An old boss jock told me years ago, "You know something? I've got to come into work every day, because if I didn't have a place to go, I'd turn into one big drunken fool!" I've often wondered if that wouldn't be true of me, too. If I didn't have to maintain a keen sense of hand-eye coordination for duck walking and tap dancing, and the stamina for four hours of daily shrieking on the show, who knows what alley I'd be lying in.

I don't want to say I'm a heavy drinker, but I have been known to walk into a bar and scream, "Jack Daniels, if you please—knock me to my knees!"

It's been years, but I still remember my very first dry martini. I was in my late twenties, and somebody said, "Grease, would you like to try a martini?" I took one look at that frosted glass with that olive spinning in it and said, "Absolutely!"

I took my first sip and that ice-cold glass stuck to my lower lip. I tilted the martini glass back and let the liquid gush down my throat. Then I took the olive between my teeth, chomped on it, and felt the olive juice and gin explode against the roof of my mouth. It was an incredible sensation. I could feel the warm buzz in my stomach. It was then that I realized I was in love.

When I get off work, I usually head immediately to a quiet little bar not far from the radio station. I've been frequenting this particular establishment ever since I moved to Los Angeles from D.C. Over the years, I've become one of the regulars.

One night about five of us were assembled there, drinking and talking. The conversation eventually turned to "The Great Beyond," and whether or not there was actually an afterlife. Several of the guys said they believed there was. A couple of others said it was malarkey. One thing led to another, and we decided, as a joke, to hold a séance in the bar.

One fellow was pretty upset, adamant about not wanting to talk to his deceased wife. Nevertheless, while he was in the men's room, I grabbed the Yellow Pages, found a medium who lived close by, and hired her to come over and conduct a séance.

When she arrived, we dimmed the lights in the bar and sat down at a big, round table. We joined hands and, just to rattle the protesting fellow, resolved to contact his dead wife, Maureen.

Sure enough, a cloud of mist suddenly filled the air and the vision of a woman's face emerged. A cold chill fell over the room as the woman began to speak in an eerie monotone:

163

"This is Maureen, this is Maureen, the wife you killed eighteen years ago. But I'm not angry. I've forgiven you because everything is better for me now. I have beauty, youth, riches. I make love to three or four different handsome men every week."

"Wow!" said her astonished husband. "That's fantastic! You're in heaven!"

"Heaven, schmeaven," the woman replied. "I've been reincarnated as that sixteen-year-old trollop you married six months ago!"

One night I was waiting for my bone-dry when I realized the guy a couple of barstools away was really knocking back the double scotches.

"You're hitting that stuff pretty hard," I said. "What's going on?"

He glanced over at me and shook his head. "Agh," he said. "My life is hell!"

I walked over to where he was sitting and put a meaty arm around him. "C'mon," I said. "What's the problem? Spill your guts."

He sighed and took a big swig of his drink. "Well," he began, "it was pretty slow at work today, so I figured I'd go home and spend some time with my wife. I went home early, walked through the door, and found another man putting the stones to her. I mean, he's sweating, she's sweating, and they're tearing it up like she and I never did. I was so angry, I walked in and punched the guy out!"

"As well you should have," I interjected.

"No," he cried, "you don't understand. After I punched the guy I realized it was my boss. I didn't know what to do, so I stupidly stammered, 'Oh, my God, Mr. Puddlemutter, it's you! You're having an affair with my wife!'

"And do you know what he said? He said, 'You didn't

think I kept sending you out of town because you were such a good salesman, did you?!'"

Another night I was idling in the bar, slowly sipping a bone-dry and reading the paper, when I overheard a discussion between three women seated nearby. They were busy complaining about the infidelities of their husbands.

"I discovered that my husband cheats on me when I found a stocking in the glove compartment of his car," the first woman said.

"I uncovered the horrible truth when a condom fell out of my husband's wallet," the second woman said. "But I got even. I took that condom and punched a whole bunch of tiny holes in it with a pin!"

At that point I heard a crash and glanced over at the table. The third woman had fainted!

Not long after the three women had paid their tab and departed, another feminine trio walked through the door and took the same booth. Well-dressed matrons in their early sixties, their faces were adorned with guilty looks.

Intrigued, I moved closer so I could overhear their conversation.

"Oh, God, I need this scotch," confided one of the gals. "I feel so guilty about yesterday. This bum showed up at my door and I gave him twenty dollars. I don't know what in the world possessed me to hand over that much money."

I know how you feel," said another woman. "I had a bum ring my front doorbell yesterday when I was cooking dinner. I got so flustered I pulled the ham I was baking right out of the roasting pan and gave it to him."

The third woman poked her head around the side of the

booth and motioned to the waitress. "Bring me a double, will you?" she requested, then she turned to face her friends.

"Yesterday," she said quietly, "I hobbled a bum."

The woman's friends were stunned. "You didn't!"

The woman smiled. "I certainly did!"

"My Lord, what did your husband say?" the two women asked in unison.

"Oh," she replied, "he just said 'Thank you,' rolled off, and fell asleep!"

A couple of nights later, two guys were sitting next to me, one on either side. Man, were they a couple of sad sacks! I tried to ignore the bad vibrations they were giving off, but I finally couldn't stand it any longer.

"What are you guys looking so down about?" I asked. "C'mon, what's wrong? It's a great night for laughing and drinking."

The guy on my left just mournfully shook his head, but his friend spoke. "It's our wives. They're too damn ugly to go home to. That's why we're in here, killing time."

"C'mon now," I said with a laugh. "They can't be *that* bad."

"Oh yeah?" said the other guy. "My wife is so ugly that the beauty parlor told her there's nothing more they can do for her."

"That's nothing," responded his pal. "My wife is so homely that when I took her to a plastic surgeon, he said the only thing he could do for her was to add a tail!"

These two were as solemn as judges. They left me with no choice but to share my philosophy on women.

"In my years on this planet," I began, "I have discovered that women are like the great continents."

The two sad sacks looked at me and scratched their heads.

"Allow me to explain," I continued. "From ages thirteen to eighteen, women are like Africa, unexplored virgin territory. From eighteen to thirty, they're like Asia, hot and neurotic. From thirty till forty-five, they're like America, fully explored and free with their resources. Forty-five to fifty-five, women resemble Europe, exhausted, though not without points of interest.

"And after fifty-five, though, they're like Australia—everybody knows it's down under but nobody gives a damn!"

Then there was the night I found myself sitting next to the rabbi from the local synagogue.

Ah, a learned man, I thought to myself, a man who has dedicated his life to studying the Torah. A man whose head is filled with great knowledge not only of the Jewish religion, but of all matters concerning the world and its inhabitants. Excited by the prospect of a provocative, intellectual evening, I engaged the rabbi in conversation.

"Tell me what weighs most heavily on your mind, Rabbi. Tell me of the great issue that concerns you."

"A very good question, my son," he said. "May I speak philosophically?"

"Sure. What's up?"

"It's December 31, and the New Year will be here in a few hours. At the same time, according to the Jewish calendar, it is the year 5768. And when the Chinese New Year rolls around again, it will be the year 4216."

The rabbi stroked his beard and gazed at me in contemplative silence. Then he spoke again. "Do you understand the significance of this?"

"I'm not sure I do, Rabbi."

And They Ask Me Why I Drink?

"I thought not," he said with a sigh of resignation. "My son, the significance of this is that we have lived without Chinese food for more than fifteen hundred years!"

On another night that the rabbi came into the bar, I decided to impress him with my wisdom.

"I would like to share a little-known fact concerning one of the most momentous events in history: The invention of the wheel. May I, Rabbi?"

"Please," the rabbi said, and took a draw on his glass of Concord grape wine.

"Once there was an inventor who realized it would be a terrific idea if rocks, dirt, and other household goods could be moved in carts. So he thought and thought about how this could be accomplished. After several years of serious pondering, he invented the wheel—only it was square.

"In those days," I continued, "they didn't have beasts of burden. They only had slaves. They would load the carts with rocks and firewood, and tether the slaves to the carts, and urge them forward. The problem was the slaves couldn't move the cart once it was loaded down, because the wheels were square. The slaves would grunt and groan, but the cart never moved an inch."

The rabbi nodded. "I'm with you, son. Go on."

"This inventor returned to his cave to devise a solution to the situation. For forty years he sat in his cave, diagramming, sketching. Then, suddenly, after decades of isolation and concentration, he solved the problem. *He invented the whip!*"

One night the door to the bar opened, and this big guy walked in. He had a beautiful girl on each arm.

"Who's he?" I asked the bartender. "He looks familiar."

The bartender laughed. "He *should* look familiar. He's the number two quarterback for the Rams."

"Right," I said. "No wonder he's got a couple of dames on his arm."

I finished my bone-dry and ordered another, just as another tall, muscular fellow walked in. He had four women on his two bulky arms.

I motioned to the bartender again. "Who's that?"

"That's the new center for the Lakers," he said.

"Well," I chuckled, "I guess he can handle four women at a time."

I was finishing my third or fourth bone-dry when the door opened yet again. In strolled a guy who was about five foot six, at least two hundred fifty pounds, and totally bald. I watched in absolute amazement as two dozen women rushed to his side, laughing and giggling.

I signaled the barkeep one more time. "Who's *that?*"

"That's Freddie Jones, the plasterer."

"Freddie Jones, the *plasterer?*" I shook my head. "I don't get it."

"I know," the bartender laughed. "I've had the same response. The only thing I can figure is that Freddie really knows how to fill a crack!"

CALLER: *How did you go get such a beautiful Funny Little Honey? And how can I get one like her?*

GREASEMAN: *Well, buddy, all you've got to do is pump up, become grotesquely overdeveloped, get yourself a major radio job, and put on a pair of python boots. A set of nine-inch hydraulics couldn't hurt, either!*

Chapter 21

Love and Its Consequences

I had all kinds of adventures when I was a Boss Jock dating man. One time I took a high-profile newswoman out to dinner. I was looking forward to the eventual slap slap slap of the doodads at the end of the evening, but we wound up spending most of the night at the dinner table.

There was no stopping her. She slopped up entree after entree, chicken and shrimp and beef and huge pasta dishes—spaghetti sauce flew all over the front of her blouse. Then she ordered a big slab of cheesecake dripping with cherry sauce for dessert. It was a hideous sight to behold!

Dinner dragged on for six hours. When we finally left the restaurant, I hailed a taxi. The cab pulled over and I gave the cabbie her address. Then I opened the back door.

"Get in," I said.

She looked puzzled. "What are you doing? Why are you sending me home?"

"Listen, lady, after all you ate tonight, I don't think there's room to stick *anything else* into you!"

One year I was on a single radio station, a year later I was broadcasting on four. Soon the show was syndicated around the country. And there I was, Johnny Avocado, duck-walking, ditty-bopping, loving life, and spreading "The Word According to Grease!"

There was only one thing missing in my life: LOVE! And then along came My Funny Little Honey, and life took a definite turn for the better.

I'll never forget the first time I saw My Funny Little Honey. I was sitting in my favorite bar, feeling depressed, owing to the lack of true love in my life. I had played the field long enough—actually *romped* is a better word—and was ready for more. More, I say!

I was sipping on my bone-dry when a rather attractive lady entered the establishment. She sat down beside me and we struck up a conversation. Just as I was revving up my charm, I discovered that she was a lesbian. Seeing as the romantic possibilities between us were severely limited, we settled for a nice chat.

Suddenly, the door swung open and this gorgeous woman strode inside, bringing the sun's light into the dark room. Both my lesbian friend and I turned to watch her.

"If only I could get my hands on those bodacious ta-tas," my new lady friend whispered. "I would rub my face in that scrumptious scamper, and keep her happy for an hour or two!"

I looked at the gorgeous woman who would soon become My Honey.

"Damn," I said. "I must be a *lesbian* too!"

And They Ask Me Why I Drink?

My Funny Little Honey and I got off to a rough start. On our first date, I went to pick her up in my prized 1966 Chevy Biscayne. She stepped out the front door, took one look at it, and refused to get in. "Too old-fashioned," she said, and went back inside the house.

Nonetheless, she looked so good I decided to go back the next day. But before I returned, I borrowed a buddy's blue '74 Mustang to really impress her.

History repeated itself. She gave the car a quick once-over and declined my invitation to get in.

"Too old-fashioned," she sneered once more.

The same thing happened when I showed up in a cherry 1976 Barracuda.

Thoroughly frustrated, I vowed to spare no expense. I went out and rented a brand-new silver Cadillac. When she walked out the door, her eyes lit up. This time, she happily got into the car.

The date went magnificently. We sipped cocktails in the moonlight, then enjoyed fine food spiced with clever banter. We ended up at lovers' lane, where our kissing was passionate, hungry, and intense.

We were both panting when suddenly she whispered, "Nino, do you want me to pull off my panties?"

"No," I replied. "Too old-fashioned. *Spit out your gum!*"

CALLER: *Hey, Greaseman, what's the Grease Palace like? Is it really fancy and opulent?*

GREASEMAN: *Well, once you get by the electrified fence, the alligator pits, the claymore mines, and the armed guards patroling with Dobermans, it's really just a house like anybody else's.*

Chapter 22

The Grease Palace

For a long time, I never knew how difficult it was to run a household. Usually I would leave all that up to My Funny Little Honey, and she would leave the finances up to me.

One day our housekeeper, Roberta, came barging into the study. I was in my smoking jacket, swirling a glass of heated brandy while contemplating the vicissitudes of life.

"Excuse me, sir," she began.

"Damn it, Roberta," I told her, "not while I'm listening to Vivaldi!"

"I'm sorry, sir," she replied, "but I was wondering if I could have the Friday after Thanksgiving off."

I looked at her in amazement. "Sit down, Roberta. There's something we need to get straight!"

I took out a pencil and a piece of paper, and began to calculate aloud. "There are three hundred sixty-five days in the year, fifty-two weeks per year. You take two days off for each weekend. That leaves two hundred sixty-one working days. You spend sixteen hours a day away from the house here, so that accounts for one hundred seventy days, leaving ninety-one days available for work. You spend thirty minutes each day on a coffee break, which adds up to twenty-three days a year.

"Now," I continued, "ninety-one days minus twenty-three days equals sixty-eight days. Sixty-eight days available for work. You spend an hour a day at lunch and that accounts for another forty-six days per year, which leaves only twenty-two days available for work. You spend two days per year on sick leave and you take nine holidays per year. That leaves eleven days available for work. You then take ten days vacation a year, which only leaves one day a year available for work.

"In conclusion, Roberta, no way are you going to take that one remaining day off!"

When My Funny Little Honey and I moved into our new Grease Palace, our hillside retreat high above the hills of Los Angeles, we wound up refurbishing it inside and out. A department store salesman asked us the kind of furniture we were interested in.

"We were thinking about purchasing some period furniture," I explained.

"What period are you interested in?" the salesman asked. "Early American? Old English? French Empire?"

I shook my head. "We want the kind of furniture," I replied, "that when our neighbors see it, they'll drop dead, *period!*"

The Grease Palace is not just my home, it's my sanctuary. Whenever I get off the air, I follow the same routine. I pump a little bit of iron in the gym, then head for home. I put on my bathrobe and sit around, doodads akimbo, while My Funny Little Honey cooks up some chow. After dinner, I pop a tape of *Buttmasters* or *Chicks with Sticks* into the VCR, and settle back in my favorite chair with a fine Mandarin Napoleon Liqueur.

And then, just when I'm calm and safe and relaxed— Bam! Bing! Bong! The doorbell rings!

Time and time again I lumber over to open the front door, and find a salesman standing there. "Hello, sir," the poor fool announces, "I'm from this or that company, and I want to sell you some newfangled piece of garbage that you don't need, and blah, blah, blah."

My reply has always been the same: *"Get out of my face!"*

One night the doorbell rang so many times I finally went over the edge.

I dragged my .870 out from behind the couch and pointed it at the door. Every time the bell rang, I fired. In this way, I watched the entire eighty-seven minutes of *Amazon Gals and Their Prison Pals* on my VCR. Before retiring for the evening, I opened the door and moved the bodies off to the side. Fortunately, there wasn't much of a mess. So many *Lighthouse* and *Watchtower* magazines were lying on the front stoop, they soaked up all the blood!

The thing I enjoy most is being home with My Funny Little Honey. However, when you're in show biz, you have to go out, at least every once in awhile, on the cocktail party circuit. I hate it, but it's something I have to do.

What bothers me most about this scene is being in a room full of strangers. Even though everybody looks normal, you never really know what's going on in their heads.

And They Ask Me Why I Drink?

For instance, I ran into this one guy at a party who was well dressed and well mannered—a regular, pleasant fellow.

When we were introduced, he stuck out his hand and said, "Hi, Grease, glad to meet you. My name's Ralph."

Man, oh, man, did that guy have a firm grip! He grabbed my hand and my knuckles started grinding.

"That's one hell of a handshake, Ralph!" I said. "What are you, a weight lifter?"

"No," he replied. "I'm a compulsive wailer!"

After encounters like that, it's especially good to escape into the sanctuary of the Grease Palace. Of course, even when ensconced at my hilltop retreat, I have to venture out a couple of times a day to walk my dog Blue.

As cute and as wonderful as he is, Blue has caused me no end of irritation.

When I first got Blue, I tried to train him in the Pavlov style of a conditioned response. Following the textbook, I taught him to eat every time I rang a bell.

I wasn't thinking about what might happen when the doorbell rang. Last week Blue ate two steaks, three biscuits, and an Avon Lady.

Still, I like to take Blue for long walks. It gives him a chance to exercise, and it offers me the opportunity to chat with my neighbors. The other afternoon, Blue and I were standing on a corner getting ready to cross the street, when a police officer drove up to us. The officer got out of his car and said, "What are you doing, buddy?"

"I'm just walking my dog. Why?"

"If you're walking your dog," he said, "why is your dog just standing there, staring at that fire hydrant?"

I looked down. Sure enough, there was Blue in point position.

"Well, Officer," I explained, "every now and then Blue gets a little philosophical. He's looking at that fire hydrant and thinking, 'To pee or not to pee?'"

While out and about with Blue, I ran into one of my neighbors, a public school teacher. Well aware of my interest in all aspects of the human condition, she told me about an experience she recently had in class.

She had asked the kids in her homeroom to stand up and explain what their fathers did for a living. Everything was going along just fine until one kid stood up and announced, "My father's a towel boy in a whorehouse."

The teacher was shocked. "That's not funny," she scolded. "Where did you hear such a thing?"

"That's what my father tells me he does."

After school the teacher called the boy's house and got hold of his father. "Sir," she began, "your son told the class today that you are employed as a towel boy in a whorehouse. Did you tell him to say that?"

"Yes," the man said, "of course I told him to say that."

The teacher was incensed. "Well," she said, "I'm afraid I don't understand why you would share that information with your son."

"Actually," he confessed, "I'm a *lawyer*. But I certainly can't have my son going around telling people *that*, now can I?!"

Leaving the Palace to drive to work the other day, I saw a buddy of mine, a very successful attorney, waiting for a bus on Sunset Boulevard. I pulled to the curb and called to him, "Why are you waiting for a bus?"

"I guess you haven't heard," he said. "My BMW was carjacked."

And They Ask Me Why I Drink?

"That's terrible! What did the police say your chances were of getting the car back?"

He sheepishly looked down at the pavement. "I haven't reported the car missing to the police yet," he said.

I was astounded. "Your BMW was carjacked and you haven't reported it to the police?"

He gave me a sly wink. "Well, you see," he explained, "*my wife* was in the car . . ."

I gave my pal a ride and continued on my way. Before going into the studio, I parked on Rodeo Drive to pick up some new clothes. I soon found myself lumbering along behind an elderly couple. As they were both hard of hearing, they were conversing rather loudly.

I was window-shopping, not really paying attention to the couple, until I heard the woman address her husband in a rather pleading voice. "Is there *anything* I can do," she said, "to make you more interested in *sex?*"

The husband looked at her and enthusiastically shook his head. "Yeah," he said. *"Leave town!"*

CALLER: *How do you keep such a positive attitude all the time, Grease?*

GREASEMAN: *I'm just a happy guy.*

CALLER: *You never get in a bad mood?*

GREASEMAN: *Almost never. Well, the time that my Vac-u-jack threw a bearing I got a little upset. Oh, and I got a little upset when I was at an orgy, and didn't realize until fifteen minutes had passed that it was my dog, Blue, who was licking my bombays.*

Chapter 23

Here Today, Possibly Gone Today

I truly am a most happy fellow. I realized years ago that you never know when the Grim Reaper is going to pay you a visit, so I face each day with a gleam in my eye and a smile on my face. I take the time to breathe deeply and savor life, because I know full well that each breath could be my last.

Even though I'm a happy, perky kind of guy, there are times when, like everyone else twirling around on this planet, I find myself bugged by the little annoyances of life. Those moments don't last long, though, because I've learned how to deal with them.

* * *

And They Ask Me Why I Drink?

Everything slammed into perspective a couple of months ago. I was standing at a street corner when a funeral procession passed by. When you're talking funeral, you're talking end of the line. As I stood there, I found myself just happy to be alive, driving The Greasemobile, loving My Funny Little Honey, doing my radio show—just loving life and being thankful for everything I had been given.

Well, the light turned red and the hearse stopped right next to me. A fellow was sitting next to the driver in the front seat, and I could tell he was the husband of the deceased. The guy was crying his eyes out, saying over and over, "I can't believe Ethel is gone! I can't believe she's gone!"

The light turned green; the hearse started to pull away. I could still hear the widower as the hearse pulled away. "I can't believe Ethel is gone! *I can't believe Ethel's in the back seat and not telling somebody how to drive!*"

Going to a funeral always takes the wind out of you a bit, especially if the service is for a friend.

The last funeral I attended was for an old buddy of mine. It was quite a shock to learn that he'd died, because he had always appeared to be in good health. One day, he just keeled over. I was there as a pallbearer, waiting for his wife to take one last look at her husband before they closed the coffin forever.

As I watched, the widow slowly approached the open coffin. She bent over and kissed her dead husband farewell, then placed several little cheese wedges in the coffin with him. I suppose that is the custom these days. If the deceased had been a cigar smoker you'd put a couple of cigars in the casket. If he'd been an avid golfer in life, you'd put a club and a couple of balls in with him for eternity.

The wife chose cheese because it represented the special times they'd shared in life. Every day when he came home from work, they had a couple of drinks and some cheese and crackers, as they discussed the events of the day. As a final remembrance, his teary-eyed little wife threw in some slices of gorgonzola.

We all filed past the casket to pay our last respects. The lid was then closed and bolted down. One of the pallbearers came rushing in late, just as the other pallbearers and I stood up. We each grabbed a handle on the casket, hoisted it up, and walked out of the church. We loaded the casket into the hearse, then we all drove to the cemetery. Again, we hoisted the casket, this time carrying it toward the grave.

God, was it hot that day! It must have been 104 degrees in the shade. As we slowly proceeded toward the grave site, I could smell the pungent odor of the warm gorgonzola.

Now I knew what the stench was, but the late-arriving pallbearer had no idea. He started sniffing the air, then suddenly he let go of his handle. *Bam!* The casket fell to the ground.

"What are you doing?" I yelled. "Why'd you let go like that, for Chrissakes?"

"Listen," he said, "if the guy in the box just did what I *think* he did, then he can also *walk* himself to the grave!"

A friend of mine had a particularly bizarre experience at a funeral. A widow had her husband cremated, then requested the funeral director put the ashes in an hourglass. He thought it an unusual request, but he followed her instructions. The hourglass was then given to the widow.

A day later, my friend went to pay his respects to the woman. While they were sitting in the living room, he noticed the hourglass on top of the fireplace mantel. The two were in mid-conversation when the woman noticed the ashes were not moving through the hourglass. She went over to the mantel, picked up the hourglass, and slammed it upside down.

"All right, you lazy SOB," she said, "for the first time since I've known you, *you're going to work!*"

Another strange story I heard concerned a man who had passed away so suddenly that the widow was constantly asked to explain the cause of death to each of the mourners.

The widow looked each of them straight in the eye. "Gonorrhea," she said.

Not knowing how to respond, the mourners would all shake their heads and silently move on.

After the widow had told about a dozen people her husband had passed away from the ravages of venereal disease, her son leaned over and whispered, "Mom, what's the deal? Why are you telling everybody Dad died of gonorrhea when he really died of diarrhea?"

Embarrassed, the woman looked down at the carpeting. "Well, son," she whispered softly, "I'd rather people think your father died a *sport* rather than the *turd* he really was!"

Given my acute awareness of the fleeting nature of life, I am aghast when I hear people talk about spending their free time thrill-seeking, such as freefall parachuting or shark hunting.

No, you won't find me up at Piscannaway Park waiting in line to bungee jump upside down, my seersucker suit pathetically flapping behind me, a racing form flying out of my pocket. Nor will you see me cueing up at the parachute jumping school.

No way. When I jump, it's in the pool after spending an afternoon with a nice book and a can of beer.

I don't need an artificial adrenaline surge. I get a rush when I invite a stimulating couple over for light banter. Or when I discover a great book. Or when I sip the perfect bone-dry. Or when someone calls up the show and says, "Grease, you changed my life."

I get a rush when My Funny Little Honey laughs as I come scooting around the corner, new story to tell. I get a rush when she's cooking in the kitchen, the lids rattling on top of the pots, the scent of intoxicating culinary delights filling the air.

So you won't find me at the latest amusement park ride that turns you upside down and causes you to heave your cotton candy. I'll be the guy sitting on the blanket watching you. I'll be the guy shaking his head in wonder at the newspaper headline—"Wife Watches as Husband Bungee Plunges to His Death!"

I'll be the guy sitting by himself looking at the sunset, watching the horizon until that glowing orange ball in the west breaks the angle of the ocean and disappears, making the end of yet another glorious day of living.

CALLER: *I was wondering if there's a cure for hemor-
rhoids.*

GREASEMAN: *Yes. Put a few piranha in your toilet
bowl.*

Chapter 24

Grease Mannelli: Planetary Advisor

People are always calling in search of advice. "Grease,"
they'll sometimes say, "why you are so sage? Where did all
your mighty wisdom come from?"

That question is easy to answer. Consider all the lives,
past and present, I've lived. Ponder the various profes-
sions in which I've dabbled. Reflect on the innumerable
skirmishes I've endured while duck-walking from one
end of this planet to the other. Who could be better at
dispensing helpful, provocative advice to the lovelorn and
the misbegotten than an experienced connoisseur of the
realities, inanities, and absurdities of life?

Forrest Gump was right on the mark when he said life
was like a box of chocolates, because you really never *do*
know what fate has in store. Opening chest cavities and
performing complex surgeries . . . spinning and pounding in a courtroom . . . weaving a tale to sell deodorant to
the public . . . I had no idea I would wind up being a Boss

Jock, with a nationally syndicated radio show. And now here I am, this year's Testosterone Poster Boy, utilizing all those experiences to entertain and enlighten you. What you hear on "The Greaseman Show" is the culmination of a life's work.

Broadcasting is more than a job—*it's a calling*—and in pursuit of my calling, I've had to transform myself into an authority on a stunningly broad range of subjects—everything from adultery to zoophobia—with a special emphasis on the ups and downs, the ins and outs, of *love*.

And so I approach the microphone each day, armed and ready, for the multitude of queries that come floating to me over the airways . . .

On dating . . .

Caller: I need your advice. I'm engaged to this girl. We've been going out a year and a half. I know all about her past and she knows about mine. I asked her who she'd slept with and now I think I regret knowing! Every time I hear one of their names I go into a frenzy. I even beat up one of the guys! I can't help it. I can't get it out of my head.

Greaseman: You're going to have to get it out of your head or your relationship is finished. Look, if I gave you a Rolls-Royce, you'd still drive it, wouldn't you? You wouldn't care that my hands had been all over it—that I'd pushed all the buttons on the radio, that my foot had caressed the accelerator, that my big *tokhis* had been sitting in the driver's seat. You'd be saying, "Oh, man, this is a great car! It makes me feel good!"

You've got to look at your girlfriend the same way. Who cares if some guy had his hands all over her. You're the guy with the hands on her now.

Caller: That's what everybody says, but I just can't get it out of my mind.

And They Ask Me Why I Drink?

Greaseman: Well, then, maybe you'd better not marry her. Why don't you go find a virgin nobody has ever zapped. Of course, sooner or later, she's going to wonder what another man is like, and then she'll break your heart. I say drive the Rolls-Royce even though a couple of other mechanics have changed the oil!

On dating revenge . . .

Caller: Three months ago, my ex-girlfriend and I celebrated our one-year anniversary. I went all out. I rented a spa and put it in the middle of a beautiful, grassy field. I filled it and plugged it in with about eight extension cords. And we did a little slicing.

Greaseman: So what's the problem, sir?

Caller: I went away on a business trip, and she did the exact same thing with another man.

Greaseman: Well, so, just because you and she enjoyed sparks in the spa doesn't mean she can't enjoy it with another person.

Caller: The point is—we weren't broken up yet.

Greaseman: Ohhhh!

Caller: Where's my revenge, Greaseman?

Greaseman: You don't take revenge. Too many people have ruined their lives trying to get revenge over a failed love. All right, you were there. You had a slice or two; don't worry about revenge. It will only be destructive. Thank your lucky stars you didn't get married and then discover she's out renting hot tubs with guys. I say *move on!*

On breaking up . . .

Caller: My girlfriend and I were going out for two and a half years. Now she's broken up with me, and I don't know how to get her back.

Greaseman: You can't get her back. She broke up with you, which means she doesn't want to see you for a while. Leave her alone!

Caller: But I'm still in love with her!

Greaseman: I know, but she's not in love with you. You've got to give her some time.

Caller: We're both away at school, and have been apart for about three months. I thought that when I came home for Thanksgiving break, we'd get back together. But she doesn't want to see me.

Greaseman: She doesn't want to see you? Don't see her. Leave her alone. Forget about her. The one way you can guarantee never seeing this woman again is by calling and harassing her. Right now she doesn't hate you, she's just a little tired of you. But if you keep on bugging her . . .

Caller: Should I find another girl to make her jealous?

Greaseman: Leave her out of it! Can't I get it through your skull? What am I talking to here, plywood? Forget about her! Write your girlfriend a letter that says, "We had some good times. I'll always treasure them. If you ever want to get together, call me." And then never call her again because if you keep on like this, you'll become fixated, possessed, and ultimately I'll be reading about you in the paper: "Spurned Boyfriend Slays Girlfriend and Her Family!"

On lust and greed . . .

Caller: I'm twenty-four and I've found a girl I really like. I was going to ask her to move in with me, but my mother won't let me.

Greaseman: You're twenty-four years old—you can do whatever you want!

Caller: Yeah, but Mom's really old and I don't want to hurt her feelings, *or* take the chance of her disowning me.

Greaseman: So the only reason you're hanging around your mother is so you get her stuff when she dies.

Caller: Well, kind of . . .

Greaseman: What a loving son you are!

Caller: I do love her, it's just that I want to do what I want to do.

Greaseman: If you love a woman and want to move in with her, move in with her. The only reason you're not is that you're hanging around like a bird of prey waiting for a rotting carcass! How old is your mother?

Caller: Seventy-six.

Greaseman: Some of these women live forever, you know. She could live to be ninety-six. Twenty years from now you'll still be waiting for the inheritance, only to find out there are all kinds of liens on the property, that her bank account is nonexistent, that she sent all her money off to some TV evangelist. By that time you'll be forty-four years old, and the woman of your dreams will have abandoned you all because you waited for a pot of gold at the end of a rainbow that doesn't exist! Think about that, sir!

Caller: Maybe I ought to ask the girl to just move in with me.

Greaseman: Do it! Maybe the shock will cause your mother to drop before she gets a chance to change the will!

On sibling rivalry . . .

Caller: Greaseman, I got a little problem. You see, my best friend is sleeping with my sister, and I don't know what to do about it.

Greaseman: How old is your sister?

Caller: She's forty-three.

Greaseman: She's a grown woman. How old is your best friend?

Caller: He's twenty-six.

Greaseman: Whoa, Nellie!

Caller: I don't understand it.

Greaseman: She's already had guys her own age. They've lied to her and cheated on her. Sooner or later she'll marry another slug her own age, but right now she's just having fun. Believe me, at age forty-three, your sister has easily been through the mill. It must be like Christmas, having this young stud taking care of her.

Caller: But she's got two children from her first marriage.

Greaseman: Two children, can't get arrested. Your friend came along and cut her a mercy slice! Take him out to dinner and buy him a big, thick steak to keep his strength up! The more he zaps sis, the happier she's going to be. You want your sister to be happy, don't you?

Caller: Not really.

On the world's oldest profession . . .

Greaseman: You're a prostitute?

Caller: Yes. That's what I do for a living.

Greaseman: Where do you do it? Where do you sell your wares?

Caller: I was on the street before, but now I'm doing it privately for an escort service.

Greaseman: How much do you charge?

Caller: It depends on what you want done.

Greaseman: How much for a normal zesty session?

Caller: Well, for you, about . . .

Greaseman: No, no, not for me! I'm asking as a public service for the people. How much does it cost?

Caller: About three, four hundred dollars.

Greaseman: Three or four hundred dollars? What have you got, a pussy lined with gold? I don't want to *buy* it—I just want to *rent* it!

On sex, this way or that . . .

Caller: I'm a college student and I've got a problem. I'm twenty-one, and have been heterosexually hobbling and gobbling all my life! But my roommate and I were drinking the other night, and we got to experimenting . . . and he gave me a snarlin'. I kind of liked it! Now I don't know what to do.

Greaseman: That's pretty intense! How do you "experiment" with a thing like that? All of a sudden, he's giving you a snarlin'? Did you reciprocate?

Caller: Yeah, kind of.

Greaseman: You gave him a snarlin' after he gave you one?

Caller: Actually, it was at the same time. I didn't even know *what* was going on.

Greaseman: You knew what was going on, all right. Don't use alcohol as an excuse!

Caller: I don't know if I'm really that way or not!

Greaseman: Well, sir, I'd say that yesterday was your Coming Out Day, and that you came out in a big way!

On marital sex . . .

Caller: Grease, I'm sixty-two but I'm married to a twenty-one-year-old girl. She is a frisky one! When we start having at it, the slap of the doodads is pretty intense. I thought maybe I could draw on your medical knowledge about this problem I'm having.

Greaseman: What's the problem?

Caller: The problem is, when we're having ingus I don't know whether I'm having an orgasm or a heart attack!

Greaseman: That's easy! If you grab your chest, it's a heart attack. If you grab her chest, it's an orgasm!

More marital sex . . .

Caller: Grease, I hear all these guys calling you up, complaining about *not* getting a slice from their women. I have just the opposite problem. My wife is a bona fide nympho, and I just can't keep up the pace. I'm afraid I'm just going to burn out completely.

Greaseman: Okay, this is what you do. Start charging her per slice. You tell her constant sex is a lot of effort on your part. You can't just lay back and enjoy it because it involves a lot of hydraulics power. So tell her you're setting up a fee system. For example, if she wants a slice on the kitchen floor, the fee will be five bucks. The living room couch, ten dollars. The hallway steps, fifteen dollars. And if she wants a true bedroom slice with all the trimmings and frills, twenty-five dollars. Trust me, when she starts running up the tab, she'll think twice about all this action!

Caller: I tried that already, Grease! Last night she reached for me hungrily, and I gave her a price list—five bucks for a slice on the floor; ten bucks, the couch; fifteen bucks, the hallway; twenty-five bucks, the bedroom.

Greaseman: So what happened?

Caller: Well, she looked at me for a minute, then she went to her purse and pulled out some money. "Here's twenty-five dollars," she said. I said, "Great. Let's go to the bedroom!" She said, "No way! I want *five slices on the kitchen floor!*"

Even more on marital sex . . .

Caller: My wife is the ten-minute woman. She achieves her Shangri-la in ten minutes. Then it's me . . . and then that's it. She says, "Okay, that's all. Good night!"

Greaseman: Well, sir, sex is like Chinese food. It's over once you get your cookies.

On marital sex . . .

Greaseman: You sound upset, sir! What's wrong?

Caller: I've been married sixteen years, Grease, and I love the woman! She's a good woman, but there's only some things she'll do . . .

Greaseman: I understand! But is it worth torching a marriage of sixteen years because your wife refuses to gobble de gee?

Caller: No, I can't get divorced. This is all I know. I go to work. I come home. That's all I do. Go to work and come home. That's all I'm allowed to do. I've got no outlet.

Greaseman: That's all any of us do, sir. We go to work and then we go home. That's our lot in life. What do you expect, popping corks and champagne dances? No. The lot in life of the working man today is you wake up, kiss your wife, go to work, finish work, and go home. Oh, perhaps you can cut an hour into the day to pump a little iron, but that's it. Other than that, it's the same routine until you die!

But you can't let it get to you. If you do, you'll wind up in the loony bin with someone saying, "Now, be a good boy, take your medicine! Oh, you didn't finish everything in the paper cup. You don't want me to have to call Big John from upstairs and have him shove it down your throat, do you?" You don't want that to happen, do you?

On infidelity . . .

Caller: I got married two months ago. When I came home one night after work, I found my wife with an old boyfriend.

Greaseman: How do you like that? Married two months and already she's double-deucing you!

Caller: Yeah, then I got a summons in the mail on charges of assault and battery against this gentleman.

Greaseman: You beat him up?

Caller: Yeah.

Greaseman: You shouldn't have done that.

Caller: What do I tell the judge when I get pulled into court?

Greaseman: You tell him what husbands have been telling judges from the beginning of time: "Your Honor, I'm sorry. If I had it to do all over again, I never would have married this woman, let alone beat up this guy. I know it was wrong, but I was momentarily blinded by rage. I throw myself on the mercy of the court."

And listen, the next time you run into your woman hobbling another guy, take out your wallet, remove a five-dollar bill, throw it on the bed, and say, "Here, buddy! Why don't you go get yourself something *decent!*"

On divorce . . .

Caller: My wife and I are headed to divorce court, and she's going to fight me for custody of my kids.

Greaseman: Here's what you need to say: "Honey, you know we're talking about divorce, but we've had some good times so that's why I want to be real honest with you. I look forward to having my freedom. I want you to have full custody of the kids. I don't mind paying the child support, even if I have to get a part-time job. The thing I'm looking forward to is happiness in a relationship again.

"Frankly," you continue, "I want to date a young girl, seventeen or eighteen, who is not as bitter and angry as you are, who hasn't been through all that you've been through. So I want *you* to have the kids because I won't have the time. I'm going to come home from work and relax. I'm going to order a pizza, sit on the couch, watch a video, and giggle with my new girlfriend. I won't have to be the chief cook and bottle washer and disciplinarian.

"Besides, you're much better at meting out punishment than I am. Also, I'm planning on taking a lot of trips, something we didn't do in our marriage. Yeah, when I find my new dream woman we'll go down to the Bahamas for the weekend, which I couldn't do if I had the kids, and we'll probably spend Christmas in Jamaica. Don't worry, though. I'll still come by and say a quick 'Hello and good-bye' to the children.

"So let's not argue over custody of the kids. I'd like you to have them and I'll pay whatever the court decides in support. I mean, hey, that's the least I can do considering you're going to have them every minute of every day. When I see them it will just be fun time."

At that point your wife is thinking, "Hey, wait a minute! I want the eighteen-year-old boyfriend. I want my freedom, too."

So, while you're still talking, she suddenly announces: "No, darling, you can have full custody of the kids! You're not pulling that one on me! You've screwed around throughout this marriage—now it's my turn. You're taking full custody of the kids, you hear me." She slams the bedroom door in your face. She doesn't see you smile. She doesn't hear you say, "*Schweet!*"

On the state of the world . . .

Caller: I'm calling because our little town's high school had its first shooting today, and I'm concerned. I guess I've been out of school too long. I don't understand what's going on.

Greaseman: I'll tell you what's going on. We've always had maggots in society, but in years gone by they generally kept to one side of town. They had no mobility. It was pretty difficult to rob someone at an ATM across town if you were traveling by public transportation.

Now, however, thanks to crack cocaine, and the huge infusion of drug money, the average maggot, the same dullard, the same dropout, the same lunatic of yesteryear, is now able to afford easy transportation and deadly weaponry. That, sir, is what's going on!

I watch the craziness that goes on, and I know that we must be getting close to Armageddon!

Caller: You ought to be on the school board.

Greaseman: Nobody listens to me. It's like whizzing in the ocean, sir!

Every day calls come in asking, "Grease, what is the meaning of life? Have you figured it out yet? What is the meaning of our existence on the planet? Is there a code, a formula, a recipe for happiness?"

I believe the answer to happiness lies in the little things in which we take pleasure, the little things that keep us smiling.

It still makes me smile to remember the time Daddy decided to buy Momma a sexy nightgown for Christmas. You know how awkward men can be when they're buying presents for a woman.

And They Ask Me Why I Drink?

Daddy told the saleswoman what he wanted. She asked if Daddy knew her size.

Daddy stood there, scratching his head, and finally came up with an answer.

"Well," he said, "when she stands in front of our thirty-six-inch TV, she blocks it out—so whatever size that is!"

It isn't much—but it's something.